Your Classroom Guide to Special Education Law

Your Classroom Guide to Special Education Law

by

Beverley H. Johns, M.S.
MacMurray College
Jacksonville, Illinois

Baltimore • London • Sydney

Paul H. Brookes Publishing Co.
Post Office Box 10624
Baltimore, Maryland 21285-0624
USA

www.brookespublishing.com

"Paul H. Brookes Publishing Co." is a registered trademark of
Paul H. Brookes Publishing Co., Inc.

Typeset by BMWW, Baltimore, Maryland.
Manufactured in the United States of America by
Sheridan Books, Inc., Chelsea, Michigan

The individuals described in this book are composites or real people whose situations are masked and are based on the author's experiences. In all instances, names and identifying details have been changed to protect confidentiality.

Cover art © istockphoto/kaisorn.

Library of Congress Cataloging-in-Publication Data

The Library of Congress has cataloged the print edition as follows:

Names: Johns, Beverley H. (Beverley Holden), author.
Title: Your classroom guide to special education law / Beverley H. Johns.
Description: Baltimore : Brookes Publishing, 2016. | Includes bibliographical references and index.
Identifiers: LCCN 2016000449 (print) | LCCN 2016016640 (ebook) | ISBN 9781598579710
    (paperback) | ISBN 9781681250267 (pdf) | ISBN 9781681250250 (epub)
Subjects: LCSH: Special education—Law and legislation—United States. | Special education
    teachers—United States—Handbooks, manuals, etc. | BISAC: EDUCATION / Special Education /
    General. | EDUCATION / Educational Policy & Reform / General.
Classification: LCC KF4209.3 .J64 2016 (print) | LCC KF4209.3 (ebook) | DDC 344.73/0791—dc23
LC record available at https://lccn.loc.gov/2016000449

British Library Cataloguing in Publication data are available from the British Library.

2020   2019

10   9   8   7   6   5   4   3   2

Contents

Contents

About the Author

Beverley H. Johns, M.S., is a Professional Fellow for MacMurray College, where she teaches courses on special education law, emotional and behavior disorders, and diverse learners. She also teaches a class on autism at Illinois College. In addition, she is a learning and behavior consultant. She is a graduate of Catherine Spalding College in Louisville, Kentucky, and received a fellowship for her graduate work at Southern Illinois University (SIU) in Carbondale, where she received a master of science degree in special education. She has done post-graduate work at the University of Illinois, Western Illinois University, SIU, and Eastern Illinois University.

Ms. Johns has 40 years of experience working with students with learning disabilities (LD) and/or emotional and behavior disorders (EBD) within the public schools. She supervised LD and EBD teachers in 22 school districts, was the founder and administrator of the Garrison Alternative School for students with severe EBD in Jacksonville, Illinois, and was later the coordinator for staff development for the Four Rivers Special Education District.

Ms. Johns is the lead author of 13 books and coauthor of four others in the field of education, including the seminal college textbook, *Learning Disabilities and Related Disabilities: Strategies for Success (13th Edition)* with Janet Lerner (Cengage, 2015). She has written her first fiction book, *Secrets of the Teachers' Lounge* (Truth Book Publishers, 2014). She wrote and appeared in a DVD for the Association for Supervision and Curriculum Development (ASCD), *Conducting an Effective IEP Meeting Connecting to the Common Core,* and wrote an online course for ASCD, *Role of the Classroom Teacher in Implementing the Common Core for Students with Disabilities.*

She has presented workshops across the United States and Canada and in San Juan, Puerto Rico; Sydney, Australia (keynote); Warsaw, Poland; Wroclaw, Poland (keynote); Hong Kong, China; Lima, Peru; and Riga, Latvia. She chaired the 10th Biennial Conference of the International Association of Special Education, held June 10–14, 2007, in Hong Kong; served as President from 2006 until January 1, 2010; and presided over the 11th Biennial Conference in Alicante, Spain, in 2009. She presented the Inaugural Marden Lecture at The University of Hong Kong in January 2006.

She is the 2000 recipient of the CEC Outstanding Leadership Award from the international Council for Exceptional Children (CEC), Past International President of the Council for Children with Behavioral Disorders (CCBD), Past President of the CEC Pioneers, Past Secretary and Governmental Relations Chair for the Division for Learning Disabilities (DLD), current Secretary for DARTS (the newly formed CEC Division for the arts and special education), and the 2007 recipient of the Romaine P. Mackie Leadership Service Award. Ms. Johns is listed in Who's Who in America, Who's Who of American Women, Who's Who in American Education, and Who's Who Among America's Teachers.

A Guide to Using This Book

Knowledge is power. People working with students with disabilities must be aware of the laws and regulations that provide protections to students, families, and educators. They must be lifelong learners and keep abreast of the laws and regulations that govern their practice. This book provides an overview of basic principles and laws that govern the field of education. It is not designed to be a reference book of all the laws and regulations for working with students with disabilities; there are several well-known texts and numerous web sites for this purpose. Rather, this book delves into the most critical laws that shape educational policy, explaining Section 504 of the Rehabilitation Act of 1973 (PL 93-112) and the Individuals with Disabilities Education Improvement Act (IDEA) of 2004 (PL 108-446). References are also made to the Family Educational Rights and Privacy Act (FERPA) of 1974 (PL 93-380), which governs the privacy of education records. This book is intended to be your guide to understanding basic education-related law as you work with a wide range of students in schools and classrooms. Reading this book is also meant to be an interactive experience in which you can apply your knowledge and think critically and creatively. Several activities, exercises, and features are included within each chapter and can be used for individual reader reflection, as part of an in-service day for educators, or as thought-provoking exercises for preservice teachers.

Each chapter introduces readers to a specific topic in special education law, opening with an overview of the core principles of the laws and regulations as well as critical court cases that provide insight into how to interpret the law. Each chapter includes a mnemonic to help readers remember key terms and ideas. Readers will also encounter a "How Would You Rule?" exercise in which they are invited to weigh in on a legal dispute in special education. After writing their answer in the space provided, they can read on to see how the court actually ruled. Every chapter also includes a comparison of two case studies depicting an everyday legal situation or challenge in special education, with one example of common mistakes made followed by an exemplary approach to handling a situation. These stories are meant to bring legal and ethical principles to light and invite you to compare and contrast effective ways to follow the law and serve students with disabilities. A list of common mistakes and solutions related to the chapter topic follows each case study comparison. Finally, each chapter ends with an Extras and Activities section that could be used for professional development, as educational activities for preservice educators, or as exercises to engage the individual reader. These extras include questions and answers related to special education law, quizzes, games, puzzles, and online activities. Readers are encouraged to interact with colleagues, reflect on the concepts discussed in the chapters, and have fun. As indicated in certain activities, see the book's answer key appendix.

That said, you will never have all the answers to the many questions that you may have about the laws and regulations. If you read this book, however, you will be given an overview of your responsibilities and gain an understanding of the key points that you must remember in working with students with disabilities. You will also learn about the mistakes that can lead to due process. This book is your go-to guide for special education law. It provides you with the knowledge that you need to act in the best interests of your students and the necessary actions you need to take to stay out of due process. Practical advice, solutions, and strategies for your daily work with students are infused throughout the chapters. In addition, a glossary of key terms related to special education law is provided; glossary terms are bold at first mention in the chapter text.

You will encounter serious topics and learn about the magnitude of your responsibility as an educator, but hopefully learning about special education law is also an engaging and lively experience. You are invited to engage with the content, strengthen your critical thinking, and make this book your own (please do write, underline, highlight, and brainstorm directly on these pages). Above all, you are called to develop a personal vision for yourself as an educator in line with the core ethical and legal guidelines governing our important work with students with disabilities.

*To the educators in our profession, who advocate
and stand up for the rights of students with disabilities and
who put the needs of students with disabilities first in their work*

*To MacMurray College, for giving me the opportunity to teach
Special Education Law and the IEP Process, and to the many
Mac students whom I have taught and who have gone out in the real
world and made a positive difference for students with disabilities*

*To Sally, one of my first students, who taught
me how important laws are in protecting the rights of
students with disabilities to a free appropriate public education*

*To Lonnie, who advocates together with
me for the rights of students with disabilities*

1

An Introduction to Special Education Law

Special education is governed by laws and regulations at the federal level and additional applicable state laws, regulations, and court cases that have established key principles guiding the education of students with disabilities. This chapter begins by providing an overview of terminology related to special education law and some basic explanation of how laws come to pass. The chapter then introduces two key federal laws in special education: the Individuals with Disabilities Education Improvement Act (IDEA) of 2004 (PL 108-446) and Section 504 of the Rehabilitation Act of 1973 (PL 93-112). Critical court cases related to special education law are also discussed.

THE BASICS OF LAW

Although it is beyond the scope of this book to spell out every detail of the laws and regulations related to special education, references to laws or regulations are included throughout so school personnel can read more about a specific area if they so desire. In this book, you will see many formal references to federal laws and regulations that apply to special education. Recognizing the meaning of these references is easy with a basic understanding of the terminology involved. A reference that includes the abbreviation U.S.C. (United States Code) indicates a law, whereas a reference that includes the abbreviation C.F.R. (Code of Federal Regulations) indicates a regulation.

A federal law is enacted when Congress passes the law and it is signed by the president. Associated regulations are then drafted within a varied time frame and sent out for public review before being finalized. Regulations are developed to help interpret and implement the law. In addition, states develop their own laws and regulations that go beyond what federal laws and regulations require; however, states that take federal dollars are not allowed to implement laws and regulations that do less than the federal laws and regulations. Besides considering federal laws, those working within special education must also abide by specific state laws and regulations and should make a point of keeping abreast of those provisions through their particular state's department of education web site and their professional organizations.

In addition to laws and regulations, several instrumental court cases have shaped the principles and policies of education. Specific questions about what laws and regulations truly mean or disagreement about how to interpret a law may occur in certain circumstances. **Parents** or school districts in these situations seek answers through due process and the courts. Several cases related to education have made their way to the Supreme Court to become the law of the land on certain issues.

Laws and regulations change, and it is important to keep current with what is happening. Educators must keep abreast of what the laws and regulations say in order to be effective. One way to do this is to become a member of local or national professional organizations, attend meetings and workshops (whether in person or online), and sign up to receive communications. School personnel may never completely understand all of the intricacies of the laws and regulations, but it is important to know where to look to find more information.

SECTION 504 AND IDEA 2004

Section 504 protects children with disabilities from discrimination because of their special needs. This law also provides **accommodations** for students with disabilities, including those who are not eligible for special education. For example, Maria is a student who has diabetes. Her diabetes does not adversely affect her educational performance, so she does not receive special education services, but she does need an accommodation plan that allows her a special diet and more frequent trips to the restroom. Craig has specific allergies to foods. His accommodation plan indicates his dietary restrictions.

In addition to protecting students, Section 504 also protects individuals who may utilize the services of a school building. For example, if the school holds an open house and an individual requires a sign language interpreter to attend the open house, then the school district must provide an interpreter. If a parent utilizes a wheelchair, then the district building must be physically accessible to the parent.

Children who have disabilities that result in an adverse impact on their educational performance are eligible for the protections of IDEA 2004. Penny has been identified as having a specific learning disability. She has difficulty processing visual information and has visual-motor problems. Her learning disability affects her ability to read and write. Jeffrey has attention-deficit/hyperactivity disorder (ADHD) and has been identified as a student needing special education within the category of other health impairment. His ADHD has an adverse impact on his educational performance. Both of these students are eligible for services under **IDEA 2004.**

Table 1.1 illustrates the differences between Section 504 and IDEA 2004. The following subsections provide a foundational understanding of these laws and regulations and define related terminology. (See a condensed summary of Section 504 and IDEA 2004 later in this chapter.) It is critical to remember that terms, laws, and regulations may change, but the overall goal is equity and access for all students so that they can have a successful, meaningful educational experience.

Table 1.1.   Comparison of Section 504 and IDEA 2004

Section 504	IDEA 2004
Disability is defined as a physical or mental impairment that substantially limits one or more major life activities, which include, but are not limited to, caring for oneself, performing manual tasks, seeing, hearing, eating, sleeping, walking, standing, lifting, bending, speaking, breathing, learning, reading, concentrating, thinking, communicating, and working (Americans with Disabilities Amendments Act of 2008 [PL 110-325]).	Thirteen different types of disabilities are specified. These disabilities must result in an adverse impact on educational performance that requires special education and related services. *Child with a disability* means a child with intellectual disabilities, hearing impairments (including deafness), speech-language impairments, visual impairments (including blindness), serious emotional disturbance, orthopedic impairments, autism, traumatic brain injury, other health impairments, or specific learning disabilities; and who, by reason thereof, needs special education and related services (20 U.S.C. Section 1401).
Comparable education and access to what other students receive	Individualized education program (IEP) based on the specific needs of the student
Accommodation plan	IEP for specially designed instruction, accommodations, and modifications
Birth through death	Ages 3–21
Accessibility for students, parents, and other consumers	Special education and related services for the student, including support for school personnel and parent counseling when necessary to provide meaningful benefit to the student

Defining Disability

Disability is defined under Section 504 as a physical or mental impairment that substantially limits one or more major life activities, which include—but are not limited to—caring for oneself, performing manual tasks, seeing, hearing, eating, sleeping, walking, standing, lifting, bending, speaking, breathing, learning, reading, concentrating, thinking, communicating, and working. Determining whether the physical or mental impairment substantially limits a major life activity is made without regard to the ameliorative effects of measures such as medication, medical devices (e.g., low-vision aids), prosthetics, or cochlear implants. It does not include the effects of contact lenses or eyeglasses (Americans with Disabilities Amendments Act [ADA] of 2008 [PL 110-325]).

There are 13 different types of disabilities specified within IDEA 2004. These disabilities must result in an adverse impact on educational performance that requires special education and related services. The term *child with a disability* is defined as a child who has intellectual disabilities, hearing impairments (including deafness), speech-language impairments, visual impairments (including blindness), serious emotional disturbance (referred to as *emotional disturbance*), orthopedic impairments, autism, traumatic brain injury, other health impairments, or specific learning disabilities; and "who, by reason thereof, needs special education and related services" (20 U.S.C. Section 1401). For a child ages 3–9 (or any subset of that age range, including ages 3–5) the term *child with a disability* may, at the discretion of the state and the local district, include a child experiencing developmental delays as defined by the state (20 U.S.C. Section 1401). This category is used when districts are not certain about the specific nature of the disability, have thoroughly evaluated the child, and wish to utilize this term until they can gain a further understanding of the child's needs.

Type of Education

A **free appropriate public education (FAPE)** under Section 504 means an education that is comparable with the education of other students. FAPE under IDEA 2004 means one that is based on the individualized needs of the student and includes **specially designed instruction** for the student (Johns, 2011). For example, a student whose disability has been identified under the category of emotional disturbance receives services under IDEA 2004 and receives an individualized **behavior intervention plan (BIP)**. That same student cannot have a stricter consequence for a behavior problem than a student without a disability. Educators must follow both Section 504 and IDEA 2004 and make sure that all students with disabilities have access to a comparable education under Section 504. If the child's disability exhibits an adverse impact on educational performance, then educators must follow the requirements of individualization required in IDEA 2004.

Multidisciplinary Evaluations

A student must receive a thorough **multidisciplinary evaluation** in order to receive special education services. Informed parental consent must be obtained. An initial evaluation must be conducted within 60 days of receiving parental consent of the evaluation, or the state may establish a time frame within which the evaluation must be conducted. The district must use a variety of assessment tools, and a notice describing any evaluation procedures that the district proposes to conduct must be provided to the parents (20 U.S.C. Section 1414). The various assessment tools and strategies utilized gather relevant functional, developmental, and academic information and include information provided by the parent. These tools assist the **multidisciplinary** team in determining whether the child has a disability and the content of the child's **individualized education program (IEP)**. Teams are never allowed to use any single measure or assessment as the sole criterion for determining whether a child has a disability or for determining the type of educational program that the student needs. The team must also use technically sound instruments that are 1) selected and administered so as not to be discriminatory on a racial or cultural bias, 2) provided and administered in the language and form most likely to yield accurate information, 3) used for purposes for which the assessments or measures are valid and reliable, 4) administered by trained and knowledgeable personnel, and 5) administered in accordance with any instructions provided by the producer of the assessment (34 C.F.R. 300.304).

When the team is determining a child's eligibility for special education, a child is not determined to have a disability if the issue is due to lack of appropriate instruction in reading or math or due to limited English proficiency (20 U.S.C. Section 1414). That is, if a math or reading program was used that did not meet the needs of an individual student, then that alone does not mean a child is eligible for special services. The team that is evaluating the student should review existing evaluation data, which includes evaluations and information provided by the parents; current classroom-based, local, or state assessments; classroom-based observations; and observations by teachers and related services providers. They then must identify what additional data are needed.

Evaluating a Student for a Specific Learning Disability Additional criteria exist for determining whether a student has a specific learning disability. The team is not required to consider whether a child has a severe discrepancy between achievement and intellectual ability in a particular subject area, but a local school district may use a process that determines if the child responds to scientific, research-based intervention as part of the evaluation procedures. Districts are now allowed to implement interventions within a **response to intervention (RTI)** or multi-tiered systems of support (MTSS) model. MTSS provides for increased levels of support for students based on their needs. A school within a district following this model implements evidence-based interventions for all students. If schoolwide interventions are ineffective for a particular student, then the school provides more intense interventions at a second level. If secondary interventions do not work, then the school will want to consider an evaluation to determine whether there is a specific learning disability.

Frequency of Evaluation Evaluations must be conducted every 3 years after it has been determined that a child has a disability and that he or she is eligible for special education services. A district shall evaluate a child with a disability before determining that the child no longer has a disability; however, a new evaluation is not required if the termination of services is due to high school graduation with a regular diploma or due to exceeding the age eligibility under state law (20 U.S.C. Section 1414).

Parental Consent As previously described, informed parental consent is required before a child receives an initial evaluation. Informed consent is also necessary prior to conducting a reevaluation unless the district can show that it took reasonable measures to get consent and the child's parent failed to respond. If the parent does not consent to an evaluation, then the school district may request a due process hearing against the parent.

There is an exception when a child is home schooled or attends a private school at parental expense. If the school district wishes to conduct an evaluation or reevaluation and the parent refuses or fails to respond to the request, then the public school may not take the parent to a due process hearing (34 C.F.R. 300.300). If the parent will not sign for placement in special education, which is required, then the school district cannot pursue a due process hearing against the parent.

Child Find Child Find is a mandate under IDEA 2004 that requires schools to evaluate any and all children ages 3–21 who may be eligible for special education services. If school personnel have knowledge of a student's disability or suspect a student has a disability, then the school has an obligation to request an evaluation of that student.

Individualization

Section 504 requires an individualized accommodation plan for a student with a disability when that disability does not adversely affect educational performance.

IDEA 2004 requires an IEP for students whose disability does affect educational performance. An IEP includes a statement of academic achievement and functional performance, goals, the special education and related services needed, and other considerations. The IEP also includes discussion of the student's progress in the Common Core State Standards (CCSS) and a plan for how the school will work to ensure the student's participation and progress in educational standards.

Free Appropriate Public Education in the Least Restrictive Environment

Under IDEA 2004, all students have a right to a FAPE in the **least restrictive environment (LRE)**. Each student is educated to the maximum extent appropriate with his or her peers without disabilities. The **IEP team** determines what that means for each individual student. One type of placement option is not appropriate for all students.

Statewide Assessment

All students must participate in statewide assessments, either with or without accommodations. A student's IEP team or the Section 504 accommodation plan team determines participation and accommodations. The IEP team must be knowledgeable about a particular assessment when considering what assessment is appropriate for the student because accommodations must maintain the integrity of the test.

IDEA and Section 504: A Summary

Key components of Section 504

- Antidiscrimination law requiring that all students with disabilities have the same access to services as students without disabilities.

- Applies to parents who have disabilities and other consumers of services provided by the public school.

- Includes any student whose disability affects a major life function.

- Provides reasonable accommodations for students with disabilities.

- Requires an accommodation plan for students with disabilities.

Key components of IDEA 2004

- Includes students whose disabilities have an adverse impact on their educational performance.

- Requires a multidisciplinary evaluation to be conducted every 3 years to determine special education eligibility. The classroom teacher is part of that evaluation.

- Once eligibility is determined, an individualized education program (IEP) is developed by a team of individuals, including the parent, the child when

(continued)

(continued)

appropriate, the classroom teacher, the special education teacher, someone who can commit services, and someone who can interpret the educational implications of the diagnostic information. IEPs are done at least once per year.

- The IEP determines the specific educational program that the student will receive and must include strengths, academic achievement and functional performance, goals for all students, special education and related services, participation in assessment, general education participation, including access to and progress in the general curriculum, and other key factors, such as a behavior intervention plan when behavior interferes with learning.

- IDEA 2004 requires that all students have a free appropriate public education (FAPE) in the least restrictive environment (LRE). LRE means that students are educated with their peers without disabilities to the maximum extent appropriate.

- IDEA 2004 requires access to and progress in the general curriculum and requires participation in statewide assessment determined by the IEP process.

KEY LEGAL RESPONSIBILITIES OF IEP TEAM MEMBERS

Now that you have an overview of the key components of IDEA 2004 and Section 504, let's look at the legal roles of each IEP team member. Remember that your role as an IEP team member is critical; the decisions you make have a direct impact on a child's access to a positive, productive school experience. The IEP has lifelong implications for a child and affects relationships with the child and parents. Planning the IEP is much more than a 30- to 60-minute period of time every year or so. The IEP helps formulate a child's educational future, so this responsibility should never be taken lightly. This chapter's mnemonic can help you remember your legal responsibilities in creating the IEP and serving children with disabilities.

One role of every IEP team member is to look for students who are having difficulties; if someone has a suspicion or knowledge that a student has a disability, then the team member must refer the student for an evaluation. Recall that this is mandated by Child Find, as defined in IDEA 2004. As previously described, many schools are implementing MTSS or RTI as a way to provide evidence-based instruction and intervention for all students. Those who do not respond well to universal, or Tier 1, instruction are offered more intense, small-group interventions, which are called Tier 2 interventions. If a student is still struggling, then the student may receive individualized, targeted Tier 3 interventions. Precautions should be taken so that students who have or are suspected of having a disability are not required to go through all the tiers of intervention before an evaluation for special education is completed. The U.S. Department of Education's Office of Special Education and

Just 3 X 5 It: A Mnemonic to Help You Remember

School personnel should CREATE an educational program that is individualized to meet the needs of the student for a free appropriate public education (FAPE).

C—Child Find: The teacher has the responsibility to seek out children who may have a disability and refer them for an evaluation.

R—Rights: Children with disabilities have a right to a FAPE.

E—Equality: Each child should equally be given what he or she needs.

A—Appropriate, access, and accommodations: Both Section 504 of the Rehabilitation Act of 1973 (PL 93-112) and the Individuals with Disabilities Education Improvement Act (IDEA) of 2004 (PL 108-446) require that the child has access to the general education curriculum and its accompanying standards with appropriate accommodations to meet his or her needs.

T—Timely: Individualized education programs (IEPs), evaluations, and progress reports all must be done in a timely fashion.

E—Evaluations: Evaluations completed by a multidisciplinary team set the stage for the IEP. The IDEA of 2004 and Section 504 are all about education for students with disabilities.

Rehabilitative Services issued a letter to state directors of special education stating that the provisions related to Child Find require states to have policies and procedures in effect to ensure that they identify, locate, and evaluate all children with disabilities and that the identification occurs in a timely manner (Musgrove, 2011). No procedures or practices can result in delaying or denying an evaluation. The letter stated, "States and LEAs have an obligation to ensure that evaluations of children suspected of having a disability are not delayed or denied because of implementation of an RTI strategy" (Musgrove, 2011, p. 1). Although there are responsibilities that all team members have in identifying students who might need special education services, individual team members have specialized roles in the IEP process and in identifying, evaluating, and monitoring the progress of students (see Table 1.2).

CRITICAL COURT CASES IN SPECIAL EDUCATION

A parent may contest a school's decision, and a due process hearing can occur when laws and regulations leave some questions unanswered or there is controversy and disagreement about what should and should not be provided by school districts. Fortunately, fewer special education disputes are escalating to due process hearings. The number of hearings nationwide declined from more than 7,000 during the 2004–2005 school year to 2,262 in 2011–2012 (United States Government

Table 1.2. Roles and responsibilities for professionals on the Individualized Education Program (IEP) team

Roles	Responsibilities
Evaluator	The classroom teacher, special educator, social worker, guidance counselor, school psychologist, speech-language pathologist (SLP), occupational therapist, and others are the evaluators included in the multidisciplinary team. The team determines the eligibility of the student for special education services.
	• The classroom teacher knows what is expected and is able to report on the child's progress toward specific grade-level achievement.
	• The social worker, school counselor, and psychologist together will know about the student's social-emotional needs. The psychologist will know about the student's intellectual ability and achievement levels. The psychologist also will know the adaptive behavior skills and will have assessed whether there is a processing deficit and whether there is a discrepancy between ability and achievement. The counselor and social worker will be aware of challenges inside and outside of the school setting.
Required IEP participant	Many people are required participants in the IEP, depending on the needs of the student. The building administrator or supervisor is the individual responsible for securing services for the student. The special education supervisor may be the one who has information about placement options. The classroom teacher is a mandated participant in the entire IEP and is required to explain the student's present levels of academic achievement and functional performance and provide feedback on potential goals and appropriate objectives. Some states require objectives for all students, whereas others only require objectives for students with the most significant intellectual disabilities, which is required by IDEA 2004. The classroom teacher also is required to provide input on student placement, related services, accommodations, assistive technology, and other factors. In addition, he or she is a required participant in the development of the behavioral intervention plan, which is created when behavior interferes with learning. Furthermore, the special education teacher comes with important information about the student's needs for special education and how he or she can provide services. The SLP brings crucial information about the importance of receptive and expressive language skills. The social worker may have a positive relationship with the parent and understand the social-emotional levels of the student. The school psychologist has critical information about the evaluation of the student. If the student has medical problems, then the school nurse provides valuable information. Whatever your role, learn as much as you can about the student's needs and share that information with the group.
IEP implementer	The IEP team determines who implements what parts of the IEP and delineates it in writing. The classroom teacher is responsible for implementing educational and support goals in the IEP for the amount of time that the student is in the classroom. The special education teacher focuses on designing effective, specially tailored strategies and accommodations for each student to meet his or her learning goals. The special education teacher should be providing assistance to the classroom teacher in how to implement those accommodations. If co-teaching is available, then the classroom teacher is working with the special educator as a team to provide services to the student. The classroom teacher differentiates instruction based on the state standards. The SLP is responsible for speech-language services. The social worker may be the liaison between the home and the parent and may provide direct services to the student. The classroom teacher is responsible for implementing the accommodations that are needed by the student.

(continued)

Table 1.2.   *(continued)*

Roles	Responsibilities
Identifying supports that staff need to meet the needs of the student	The IEP team discusses not only the needs of the child but also supports for school personnel. This is a required component of the IEP. For example, if the teacher of a student with autism believes that he or she needs more training in understanding the child's sensory issues, then the teacher should convey these concerns during the IEP meeting so that professional staff training can be written into the IEP. The special education teacher or SLP may also need additional supports to better meet the needs of the student.
Monitoring the progress of the student	All team members are responsible for monitoring the progress of the student. If the student is not making progress as expected, or if changes such as decreased school attendance or work refusal are occurring, then team members have an obligation to request a new IEP meeting before the student falls further behind. Some team members are engaged in progress monitoring and are observing how the student is performing or how the student is interacting with other students. They might notice changes in behavior. Team members see first hand whether work is too difficult for the student to complete and notice whether the student has a short attention span. Team members who see that the student is having difficulty have the responsibility to inform the administrator and ask for assistance from others. All requests for assistance should be documented in writing. Students receiving special education services should meaningfully benefit from the services, and if this is not happening, then team members have an obligation to request a new IEP meeting to discuss and problem-solve concerns.

Accountability Office, 2014). The data from the Government Accountability Office in 2014 showed a steep decline in cases in New York, Puerto Rico, and Washington, D.C., which are the areas that accounted for more than 80% of the nation's hearings. This reduction in hearings is due to efforts to rely more on mediation and resolution meetings (U.S. Government Accountability Office, 2014). Some cases may get resolved through legal settlements.

The number of cases varies in each state and district, depending on proactive strategies that districts have in place. There are few due process hearings in states in relationship to the number of students who receive special education services, but even one hearing can be very time consuming for all parties. One party will generally prevail in a hearing, whereas the other will not, and the case can slowly work itself through the court system unless the party who loses accepts the ruling and moves on to implement the decision. A few cases have made their way to the Supreme Court since the inception of the Education for All Handicapped Children Act of 1975 (PL 94-142), and those decisions guide what we do across the United States. Some of the significant Supreme Court cases and the resulting guidance are explained in Table 1.3.

Other cases did not make their way to the Supreme Court but still are significant. One such case has provided guidance on the LRE. The court used a four-prong test in *Sacramento City Unified School District Board of Education v. Rachel H.* (1994) to determine that Rachel Holland, a student with intellectual disabilities, could be served in a general education classroom (see Figure 1.1). The education of Rachel Holland would not disrupt the education of other children, and she could gain meaningful academic and nonacademic benefit from being in the general education classroom. Cost was not prohibitive for the school district.

Table 1.3. Select Supreme Court cases related to education

Decision and implications for school district personnel	Supreme Court case
Schools must provide educational benefit for students but do not have to guarantee that the student reaches his or her full potential.	*Bd. Ed. Hendrick Hudson Sch. Dist. v. Amy Rowley* (1982)
Schools must provide clean intermittent catheterization.	*Irving Indep. Sch. Dist. v. Amber Tatro* (1984)
If the proposed education plan is deemed to not meet the child's specific needs, then schools may have to reimburse a parent for private school tuition, even if the parent unilaterally places the child in the private school.	*Burlington Sch. Comm. v. Mass. Dept. Ed.* (1985)
Parents who withdraw their child from a public school and enroll their child in a private school because the school is not providing a free appropriate public education (FAPE) are entitled reimbursement if the student receives a FAPE in the private school.	*Florence County School District Four v. Shannon Carter* (1993)
Schools may have to reimburse a parent for a private school if the parent places the child in the private school, even if the child has never been enrolled in the public school.	*Forest Grove School District v. T.A.* (2009)
Schools can suspend students with disabilities up to 10 days per year.	*Honig v. Doe* (1988)
Public schools can pay for a sign language interpreter on the grounds of a parochial school.	*Zobrest v. Catalina Foothills School Dist.* (1993)
School districts are responsible for any medical services other than what a physician would perform. Districts must fund related medical services so the student can have meaningful access to the school.	*Cedar Rapids Community School Dist. v. Garret F.* (1999)

Clyde K. and Sheila K. individually and as guardians for Ryan K. v. Puyallup School District (1994) involved a student with disruptive behaviors and also used the four-prong test to determine LRE. The parents wanted the student, Ryan, in a general education class with a personal aide. The district wanted him in a specialized setting. The Ninth Circuit Court ruled that the specialized setting was the LRE for Ryan. Using the four-prong test, the court ruled that the disruptive behavior was significantly impairing the education of other students and that the third prong of the test (i.e., Will there be a detriment because the student is disruptive, and will

Four Prong Test to Determine Least Restrictive Environment

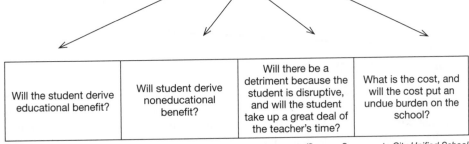

Will the student derive educational benefit?	Will student derive noneducational benefit?	Will there be a detriment because the student is disruptive, and will the student take up a great deal of the teacher's time?	What is the cost, and will the cost put an undue burden on the school?

Figure 1.1. Four-prong test to determining least restrictive environment. *(Source: Sacramento City Unified School District Board of Education v. Rachel H.* [20 IDELR 182], 1994.)

the education of the student take up a great deal of the teacher's time?) took precedence (Lerner & Johns, 2015).

There is room for subjectivity and debate when applying the letter of the law to real life, and it often happens, regardless of how clearly laws and regulations are spelled out. The following exercise invites you to think critically about situations that invite debate in special education law and apply what you have learned in this chapter to real-life situations addressed in the courtroom. Use the space provided to write your answer of how you would proceed, then look to see the real court rulings. Do you agree with the results?

How Would You Rule?

A parent was sick and asked the department of education to reschedule an IEP meeting for later in the week if he recovered from his illness. The department denied this request, believing that it had to meet the annual review deadline and therefore needed to move ahead with the meeting. Otherwise, the IEP would not meet the yearly requirement for review. Is it more important to have the IEP within the specified time or to have **parent participation**?

Your ruling:

_____

_____

_____

_____

_____

The court's ruling:

The Ninth Circuit Court ruled in *Doug C. v. State of Hawaii Department of Education* (2013) that the department of education denied a FAPE to a student with a disability by denying the parent's request to reschedule the IEP meeting because the parent was ill. The department should have attempted to accommodate the parent. The court ruled that the district was faced with the dilemma regarding two procedural requirements—parent participation in the IEP versus compliance with the IEP deadline. The department should have considered both and investigated which of the two would be more likely to deny a FAPE. The court believed that the department could have continued services for the student, even though the annual review date had expired. The fact that the parent had not refused to participate but just asked for a delay until he got well was important to the case. This case stressed the importance of parental participation in the IEP (Slater, 2014).

CASE STUDY COMPARISON

Compare and contrast the following two case studies of school systems' procedures regarding students with disabilities. First, read about an example of missteps and mistakes made in following IDEA 2004 and then read an exemplary approach to following the law and providing support for all students.

A Case of Missteps and Mistakes

Mrs. Bell is a second-grade teacher with a new student in her class this year who moved from another district. Georgie is unable to sit in his seat for more than 2 minutes. He is impulsive, jumping out of his seat, hugging other students, and making loud noises. Mrs. Bell calls his previous district because she thinks Georgie must have received some type of special education services. The principal in the previous district reports that the mother had written a request for an evaluation in January for her son. School personnel did not do the evaluation because they wanted to try more interventions. They tried Tier 1 interventions and some Tier 2 interventions during the first semester because Georgie was very disruptive. They suspected that Georgie had a disability, but school policy prohibited an evaluation when the student is in first grade. Georgie moved at the end of the year, and the evaluation had not been done. Mrs. Bell asks whether anything they tried had helped Georgie, and the principal states that none of the interventions they attempted were successful.

Mrs. Bell reports this conversation with Georgie's previous principal to her school's principal, Mr. Everett. They call in the social worker and ask the social worker to observe Georgie. The social worker observes Georgie and confers with Mrs. Bell and Mr. Everett, saying that she suspects Georgie has ADHD. All three of them believe that Georgie probably should be receiving medication. Mrs. Bell is concerned about the serious disruptions that Georgie is causing in her classroom.

They decide to call Georgie's mother in for a conference. She again asks for an evaluation of her child. She explains that she asked for an evaluation before and the school district would not do it. Mr. Everett states that he thinks Georgie may have ADHD and should be receiving medication, but Georgie's mother says that she does not want her son taking medication. The principal explains to her that the district will not conduct an evaluation until she has him evaluated by a physician for medication. In addition, the school will have no choice but to start suspending Georgie when he becomes disruptive. Georgie's mother leaves in tears. When she gets home, she picks up the telephone and calls an attorney.

What errors were made in this example? Consider the following list of missteps and mistakes:

- The previous district can be faulted for failing to complete an evaluation when personnel suspected that Georgie had a disability. There was a major problem with the district policy that prohibited a student in first grade from being referred for an evaluation. Personnel had been providing tiered interventions, which was reasonable, but those tiered interventions were unsuccessful for Georgie after an entire year of implementation.

- The previous district personnel failed to provide written documentation to the parent that they were not completing an evaluation, even though the parent had provided written permission for an evaluation. Furthermore, the previous district failed to provide information about the request for the evaluation to the new district. The new district had not received the written permission for the evaluation.

- The new district staff were correct in attempting to reach the previous school district to see what had happened during Georgie's first-grade year. When a student transfers to a new school district, the receiving school must complete assessments as quickly as possible. The new district personnel made a major mistake, however, when they told the parent that they would not evaluate Georgie until he started taking medication. IDEA 2004 expressly prohibits school personnel from requiring a parent to obtain a prescription for medication in order for the child to attend school, receive an evaluation, or receive special education (34 U.S.C. Section 1412 [c][25]).

What should the school system have done differently in this situation?

- The district personnel had an obligation to conduct an evaluation when they suspected a disability, so they should have immediately evaluated Georgie.

- The previous district staff should have provided written **notice to the parent** about why they did not evaluate the student.

- The new school district should have contacted the previous school district to get records. The previous district had the responsibility of contacting the new district if it did not receive that information.

- If the school believed the child needed medication, then the district should have recognized that the child may have a disability and conducted an evaluation.

The Exemplary Approach

Mrs. Jenkins is a fifth-year principal in an urban school district. She has never had a due process hearing filed in her school district because she strives to communicate positively with the parents of the students within her school. She makes a point of reaching out to 10 or more students in her school (more than 700) via a handwritten note or a telephone call home once a week. She also asks all of her staff to do the same thing.

Team members share through regular and honest communication when there is concern about a student. When the team of individuals believes that a referral for a student should be made for special education consideration, the principal, social worker, and teacher make a home visit to discuss their desire to help the student. At the beginning of the school year, Ms. Green, a first-grade teacher, communicates that she suspects one of her students, Robert, might have significant attention and concentration problems. Robert has trouble staying seated in class and often speaks out without raising his hand. She, Mrs. Jenkins, and the social worker immediately meet with Robert's mother to discuss evaluating Robert for special education and making a plan to help him succeed. Robert is evaluated and diagnosed with problems in attention and concentration, which results in development of an IEP and special education services under the category of other health impaired.

The school has a parent resource center where parents can come in for a cup of coffee, check out books, or utilize a computer to search for needed resources for their child. The building also has a room that can be utilized by outside agencies that need to meet with students or their families. The building is a very welcoming environment. The principal meets with school staff prior to the beginning of the school year and includes information about the important role they play as members of the IEP team, encouraging them to get to know the students and their families and help establish school as a help-ful, welcoming environment.

Mrs. Jenkins stresses that all staff are expected to be on time for IEP meetings, and she does not allow interruptions during the meeting unless there is an emergency. IEP meeting time belongs to the child and the family and takes priority. She is prepared, reviewing information about the child's background and needs before entering the IEP meeting; she expects her staff to do the same. She allows at least an hour for each IEP meeting; if the team believes the IEP will take more time, then she does not schedule another IEP meeting after that one. On a quarterly basis, she sits down with staff members who have participated in an IEP meeting to review procedures and see if there is any way that they can improve communication with parents.

Mrs. Jenkins frequently solicits questions and comments from the parents through-out the IEP process. She offers the parents coffee during the IEP meeting. She also offers transportation for parents who may not be able to attend the IEP meeting otherwise.

Mrs. Jenkins models the importance of the team process and positive relationships with parents. She goes into the IEP meeting with an open mind, determined to do what is appropriate to meet the needs of the student.

SOLUTIONS TO COMMON MISTAKES

Here are some common mistakes that special educators might make in regard to special education law, followed by suggested solutions.

Mistake: Misquoting the law or regulations when asked a question by parents or colleagues

Solution: You may not have the exact answer to the question regarding the law, but it is not advisable to fake an answer. You lose credibility with others. If you do not know the answer, say that you are unsure and that you will look up the answer. Then research the correct answer.

Mistake: Relying on other individuals' knowledge of the law, regulations, or pend-ing legislation when you are unsure of their credibility

Solution: A colleague might quote the law, regulations, or a bill that is pending. Should you believe what he or she says without checking out the information for yourself? One option is to ask the individual for the specific citation in the law or regulation. When in doubt, check it out. If you find that the individual mis-quoted the law, regulation, or proposed legislation, then you will want to store that information for future reference and know that you have to check out the information that individual gives you for yourself. For example, within the past year I received an e-mail alert noting how a piece of state-level legislation was pending and that I should support the legislation. I was suspicious and read the legislation, and there was an entire section that was harmful to a large group of educators, including me. I pointed it out to the sender of the e-mail, who became indignant, claiming that he was right and I was wrong. Rather than arguing with the individual, I simply sent him the exact wording of the legislation so he could read it himself.

Mistake: Failure to take your responsibility seriously in the evaluation or placement process

Solution: Prepare well for your role in the evaluation or placement process. Never look at the process as a nuisance but, rather, as a serious obligation that involves the future of a child. Take the time to review records, prepare assessment information, and explore all possible placement options for the student based on his or her individual needs.

CHAPTER SUMMARY

Chapter 1 introduced the basics of special education law, specifically Section 504 and IDEA 2004. You have learned about the necessity of providing a FAPE to every child, regardless of his or her disability; each team member's legal responsibilities regarding the IEP; and the importance of the court systems in answering questions or resolving conflicts that arise from special education law. This chapter also touched on the critical role of parents in educating children with disabilities and the legal requirement to have parents involved in this process. Chapter 2 discusses more about the educator–parent partnership, a relationship that is essential for planning a child's educational future.

Chapter 1 Extras and Activities

How to Advise? Tackling the Tough Questions in Special Education Law

Q: A psychiatrist has diagnosed my 8-year-old child as having bipolar disorder. My child is struggling with physical aggression within the classroom and on the playground. I do not know whether I should ask for an evaluation for my child or whether I should just wait to see if his behavior improves. I am reluctant to share the information about the evaluation with the school district because I am afraid that they will use the information against my son. I am just not sure what I should do. Should I share the evaluation that I had done independently? Does the school district have to recognize this independent evaluation, or should the district conduct its own evaluation? Can the district use this independent evaluation against my son?

A: Provide a copy of the independent evaluation to the school district personnel. Accompany the evaluation with a letter to the school principal saying that you have enclosed this independent evaluation and request a meeting by the school to recognize the evaluation. The school district must recognize and consider the evaluation; however, the school does not have to accept it. You should ask questions about your child's eligibility for services under Section 504 at a meeting in which the evaluation is recognized. Your child can benefit from accommodations. You also need to voice your concerns about the need for an evaluation done by the school district. If you want an evaluation completed by the school district, then you should make that request in writing to the school district and keep a copy for yourself. By law, the school district cannot use the independent evaluation against your child. It can use the information to assist your son in doing well at school. This is beneficial information that should be utilized to develop an appropriate plan for your son.

How Many of These Acronyms Do You Know?*

FAPE _____

LRE _____

IEP _____

IDEA _____

BIP _____

Wheel of Fortune Game*

You can play this as a team game or individually. Only a few select letters are filled in for these terms related to special education law. Fill in the rest of the letters Wheel-of-Fortune style or guess the whole term.

1. __ u __   __ __ __ __ __ __ __ __

2. __ __ a __ __   __ __ __ __ __ __ __ __ __ __ __ __

    __ __ __ __ __ __ __ __ __

3. __ r __ __   __ __ __ r __ __ r __ __ __ __

    __ __ __ __ __ __   __ __ __ __ __ __ __ __ __ __

4. __ __ __ o __ __ o __ __ __ __ o __ __

5. __ __ d __ __ __ __ __ __ __ __ __ __ __

6. __ i __ __ __ i __ i __ __ __ i __ __

Online Activities

WebQuest: Locate a court case dealing with LRE. Describe the case, facts of the case, and findings of the case. Write a summary about whether you agree with the case. Defend your position.

Two Truths and a Lie*

Read all of these statements. Two are true, and one is a lie. Determine which one is a lie.

1. The IEP not only determines what the individual child needs but also what supports the teacher may need.

2. According to the Supreme Court in *Honig v. Doe* (1988), schools can suspend students with disabilities for 10 days each time the student is suspended.

3. Schools are expected to provide any medical services other than what a physician would be required to provide.

*Answers for activities noted with an asterisk are provided in the Answer Key for Extras and Activities appendix.

2

The Parent–Educator Partnership

A Critical Ingredient for Student Success

The parent–educator partnership is a cornerstone in providing special education services. Most parents want their children to have a successful experience in school. They want to ensure their child's well-being both at home and at school, and they may be anxious about what is right for their child. School staff who provide support to parents can alleviate some of the parents' anxiety. Cooperation and teamwork between parents and school personnel are keys to a successful plan for the student. Ideally, everyone is in harmony working for a common purpose—to meet the needs of the child. This positive working relationship with parents is also critical to special education law because it can prevent due process.

Due process happens as a result of a disagreement between parents and educators. Both parties want what is best for the child in almost all cases, but they cannot agree on how to meet this goal. A breakdown in communication happens because of their disagreement. Frustration occurs when one party cannot get the other party to see what the child needs from his or her point of view.

Disagreements can be prevented when school personnel monitor their behavior and look for clues that a parent may be dissatisfied with an action being taken by school personnel. Telltale signs show when a parent is not happy with how things are going, and school personnel need to intervene at that point before the dissatisfaction escalates. Body language and personal interactions show obvious signs of concern, frustration, confusion, or unhappiness and can include facial expressions, limited responses to questions, crossed arms, avoiding eye contact, not paying attention in meetings, lack of cooperation, and so forth. Educators need to try to be cooperative and understanding in an effort to avoid a situation in which a parent is this upset. Following are some behaviors that educators can try to practice when meeting with parents:

- Being focused on the issue at hand (avoid checking e-mail or cellular telephone or talking about unrelated issues)

- Being on time

- Taking care not to interrupt

- Listening carefully and then proposing solutions that incorporate parents' ideas as much as possible

- Sending positive notes home (vs. only negative notes when there is a problem or behavioral issue)

COLLABORATING WITH PARENTS

Careful attention to behavior, demeanor, and outlook can be crucial in building a positive teacher–parent partnership. Use Figure 2.1 as a checklist for how to effectively interact and work with parents.

It is important to listen to, validate, and consider parent concerns. Our pride may get in the way at times, and we become set in our view and do not see the parent's side of the situation. We believe that we are doing our best and that the parent is being unreasonable. The parent believes that he or she knows what is right for the child, and we believe we are doing what is right. The fact is, both the parent and the classroom teacher have special knowledge of the student, so a collaborative team effort is the best way to ensure positive outcomes for the child.

Empathy is another key ingredient to interacting with parents. We may sometimes judge the parents without seeing their viewpoint. Our judgment may be clouded because of previous information we have received about the parents. It is important to understand that parenting a child with a disability can be stressful to the parents and the entire family. It is important to remember that every family experiences stress. It might be easy for us to criticize the parents for their actions pertaining to the student, but it is important to try to imagine and appreciate the responsibilities of raising a child with a disability. The parents are responsible for every aspect of their child's care, and they may work as well. Unless we take the time to visit the family at home or try to get to know them better, we have no idea what the parents have to manage each day. So, if parents show up to a meeting after school and seem angry or frustrated, consider that they may be feeling overwhelmed by larger life issues and try to practice patience.

A Checklist for Monitoring Our Own Behavior When Working with Parents

Am I actively listening to the needs of the parents and their concerns?

Am I empathetic? Do I try to put myself in the place of the parents to understand their needs and frustration?

Am I rereading everything I send home to parents to ensure that the content is not misunderstood and is constructively worded?

Am I soliciting feedback from the parents and incorporating that feedback in everything I am doing?

Am I monitoring my behavior to ensure that I keep calm and do not take comments personally?

Am I positively reinforcing the parents for their cooperation?

Am I letting the parents know when their child has had a good day at school?

Am I respecting the family's culture?

Figure 2.1.   Checklist for working with parents.

Allowing parents the time to comfortably state their concerns, ask questions, or share ideas is also critical to a collaborative relationship. Martin and colleagues (2006) observed 109 middle and high school IEP meetings and found that special education teachers talked 51% of the time, whereas family members talked 15% of the time. This does not give parents the opportunity to voice their concerns and share necessary information. Developing a sense of trust and openness is needed to truly collaborate with parents, and that can be accomplished by exhibiting flexibility, patience, humor, and active listening (McNaughton & Vostal, 2010). Active listening involves paying close attention to what is being said and to the feelings behind what is being said. Joshi, Eberly, and Konzal (2005) conducted a teacher survey and reported that face-to-face conferences were one of the best ways to meet the needs of parents who are culturally diverse.

Just 3 X 5 It: A Mnemonic to Help You Remember

It is important to treat families with RESPECT.

R—Relationships: Successful work with parents requires establishing a positive relationship by respecting what the parents are saying and by actively listening to what the parents say.

E—Empathy: Teachers must be empathetic to the needs of parents and make an effort to know the parents and consider their perspective.

S—Sincerity: Teachers must be sincere in their work with parents. They must show parents that they are genuinely interested in working with them to meet the needs of their children. Teachers must convey a deep interest in helping the student.

P—Partnership: Teachers must view themselves in partnership with the parents. They must practice a collaborative partnership with the parents by recognizing that the parents know more about the child than they do and that they can work together to meet the child's needs.

E—Effort: Trust and partnership with parents requires effort on the teacher's part. It may be that the parents have not had a positive history with school personnel or that they are new to the community. In these cases, teachers will have to put forth extra effort to meet the needs of parents and students.

C—Cooperation and collaboration: Teachers must cooperate with parents and go the extra mile to learn about what the parents want for their children. They must build on the strengths of the parents and recognize that their work with parents is the key to the child's success.

T—Trust: Trust is the cornerstone of effective relationships with parents. It must be earned by teachers standing by their word and being open to the needs of the parents.

Considering cultural differences is also critical because families come from a variety of backgrounds. Parents who are culturally diverse may have had negative experiences with schools in the past because of language barriers and can have difficulty with the printed materials that may be used by schools to share information. Consider sharing printed materials in a variety of formats—in text, using images or pictures, or as lists. This is also helpful for families who have low literacy skills.

Finally, we should monitor our communication when working with parents. Communication involves nonverbal, verbal, and written skills. Our body language should be inviting and accepting, and our facial expressions should be positive when meeting with parents. Verbal communication should also be respectful and open, and it should involve active listening and recognizing the parents' viewpoints and feelings. We should invite parents to share their views, encourage parents to give examples of what they mean, and paraphrase what we believe was said (Evans, 2004). Written communication should be clear, nonjudgmental, and factual. This chapter's mnemonic is a reminder of the best ways to communicate and work with families.

BASIC PRINCIPLES OF LAWS AND REGULATIONS REGARDING PARENTS

Under the law, the term *parents* refers to biological or adoptive parents of a child, a foster parent unless state laws and regulations prohibit a foster parent from acting as a parent, a guardian authorized to act as the child's parent, an individual acting in the place of a biological or adoptive parent with whom the child lives, or an individual who is legally responsible for the child's welfare. It can also be a surrogate parent who has been appointed by the state when a child has a natural parent who cannot be located or a child is a ward of the state (IDEA regulations 300.30). The state's department of education will appoint a surrogate who acts in the place of the natural parent. For example, a child might be placed in foster care and is in the custody of the state; therefore, a surrogate would need to be provided.

Parental involvement in evaluations and **parental involvement in placement** are critical. Parents are an integral part of the evaluation and placement process in special education and must give informed consent for an evaluation and placement to occur. Consent for an initial evaluation is not to be construed as permission for placement. If the parent does not give consent for an evaluation, then the district may pursue a due process hearing (see Chapter 1; IDEA regulations 300.300).

Parent-informed consent happens when the parent is fully informed of all information relevant to the suggested evaluation, placement, or activity in his or her native language or through another mode of communication. For example, if a specific placement is recommended for a child, then the parent must be presented with all of the information regarding that placement, including where it is located, how many students are in the class, and the type of **supervision** or instruction provided. School personnel may want to suggest that the parent visit the physical site of the placement before the parent gives consent. For an evaluation, the parent should be given an idea of what types of evaluation instruments will be utilized and who will be involved. The parent should understand and agree in writing to the activity before it is carried out, and the written consent should describe the specific activity and list any educational records that will be released and to whom.

Parents must understand that granting consent is voluntary and may be revoked at any time. If the parents revoke consent, then that revocation is not retroactive, meaning that it does not negate an action that has occurred after the consent was given and before the consent was revoked (IDEA regulations 300.9).

Informed parental consent is also required before the initial provision of special education and related services to the child. If the parent fails to respond or refuses to give consent for placement, then the school district cannot utilize due process to gain consent. The district is unable to place the student and is not required to convene IEP meetings.

Parental consent is not required before reviewing existing data as part of an evaluation or a reevaluation or administering a test or other evaluation that is administered to all children unless consent is required of parents of all children before administration of that test or evaluation (IDEA regulations 300.300).

The parent is a required member of the IEP team. Each public school must take steps to ensure that one or both of the parents of a child with a disability are present at each IEP team meeting or are afforded the opportunity to participate. These steps include notifying parents of the meeting early enough to ensure that they have an opportunity to attend and scheduling a meeting at a mutually agreed-on time and place (IDEA regulations 300.322). Parents must be provided with **prior written notice** concerning "the purpose, time, and location of the meeting and who will be in attendance." (34 CFR 300.322). If parents cannot attend the IEP team meeting, then the school district must use other methods to ensure parent participation, such as conference calls. A meeting can be held without parents if the district is unable to convince the parents that they should attend. The district must, however, keep a detailed written record of its attempts to arrange the mutually agreed-on time and place (IDEA regulations 300.322).

The district must take whatever action is necessary to ensure that the parents understand the proceedings of the IEP meeting, including arranging for an interpreter (IDEA regulations 300.322). The team must discuss any **parental concerns** regarding the education of their child during the development of the IEP (IDEA regulations 300.324). The parent must be given a copy of the child's IEP at no cost.

Parent counseling and training is a required component to consider in related services (e.g., speech-language therapy, physical therapy, occupational therapy). This means assisting parents in understanding the special needs of their child. It includes providing parents with information about child development and helping parents acquire the necessary skills that will allow them to support the implementation of their child's IEP or individualized family service plan (IFSP). An IFSP is a plan for early intervention services for young children ages 0–3 with developmental delays and becomes the IEP when the child turns 3 (IDEA regulations 300.34).

Parents have the right to an **independent educational evaluation**. This is known as the **parental right to an independent evaluation at public expense.** If they request such an evaluation, then the district must decide whether it will pay for the independent evaluation or whether it will file a due process hearing to show that its evaluation is correct (IDEA regulations 300.324). Parents must also be provided with a copy of their **procedural safeguards,** and parents have a right to a due process hearing if they do not agree with any of the special education actions taken by the district (IDEA regulations 300.504). **Parent-initiated evaluations** occur when a parent seeks out an independent evaluation at their own expense. When that occurs the school district must hold a meeting to recognize the evaluation; they don't have to accept it but they must recognize it.

This chapter's How Would You Rule? exercise invites you to think about how the school should ideally respond to parental concerns.

How Would You Rule?

A 6-year-old child was enrolled in a private school after a negative experience at his public school. After 2 years in the private school, the school district proposed that the student have a new case study evaluation in order to be moved back to the previous public school. The parents voiced concerns that the child had a high degree of anxiety from his experience at the public school and was upset at the thought of going back. He would even cry when the parents drove by the school. The district did not address this issue in the evaluation, however, because it had no data to support an anxiety disorder. Should the student have been evaluated based on the parents' comments?

Your ruling:

_____

_____

_____

_____

_____

_____

The court's ruling:

The hearing officer in *Nalu Y. by Patty and Lee Y. v. Department of Educ., State of Hawaii* (2012) ruled that the district should have assessed the student in the area of his anxiety based on the parents' concerns before returning the child to the school because the student feared the school, which was substantiated by the parents and the private school teacher.

CASE STUDY COMPARISON

As previously discussed, communicating effectively with parents requires practice and thoughtful effort. The first case study shows how communication with parents might break down and proposes some solutions. An example of an exemplary approach to interacting with parents follows, demonstrating open communication built on trust and respect.

A Case of Missteps and Mistakes

Mr. Jones works with students in a cross-categorical special education class. He believes in home-to-school journals and explains to the parents that he has purchased a notebook for each of his students and will be sending the notebook home with each child every day. The notebook will summarize what the child did that day. He asks that the parents read the notebook and write something in it about what the child did in the evening. He explains that he wants the parents to know the activities that have occurred throughout the day so that the parents can talk with their children about what they did at school. He also wants them to share family activities that he can discuss individually with the child.

Mr. Jones is faithful about sending the notebook home the first month of school, but he does not always get the notebook sent home during October and November. A few of the parents are not happy that they are not consistently getting the journal because they are conscientious and always send it back.

Mr. Jones is having some particular difficulty with Joshua and decides that Joshua's journal should be a priority. He starts reporting Joshua's behavior to the parents in late October. Mr. Jones keeps data on the number of times each day that Joshua is talking out, swearing, and hitting other students. He concentrates on these behaviors and reports the numbers when he sends the journal home. The parents become very upset because they have not heard from Mr. Jones for almost a month, and now they are getting a report that is filled with Joshua's behavior problems.

What errors were made in this example? Consider the following lists of missteps and mistakes:

- Mr. Jones should not have promised the parents something that he could not deliver, specifically a daily home-to-school journal.

- Mr. Jones should not have changed the focus of the daily home-to-school journal. He told the parents that he would be using the journal to let the parents know about the activities of the school day so they could discuss those with their child. He then turned the journal into a behavioral summary for Joshua.

What could Mr. Jones have done differently in this situation?

- Mr. Jones should have thought ahead about what was realistic for himself. Perhaps he could not do a daily note for every student but could do two a week for each student. He could stagger the notes so he did not have to complete them all on one day. He gained trust from the parents when he said he would be sending home a journal that would outline the activities of the day, and although he was able to fulfill his promise during the month of September, he could not do so in October. It is important not to make unrealistic promises to parents. I remember sitting in an IEP meeting in which a group of high school teachers all said they would send a daily note home about how a student was doing. I asked the teachers whether they could really do this considering the amount of activity that occurs at the end of the school day. The teachers insisted that they could and would do it. Teachers were not sending the note home within the first 2 weeks of the plan, and the parents were very upset. A new IEP meeting had to be convened to determine how often notes could be sent.

- If Joshua was having behavioral concerns, then Mr. Jones should have asked the parents to come in for a conference to discuss how they could work together to improve Joshua's behavior.

The Exemplary Approach

Mrs. Holden has always strived hard in her 12 years in education to establish a partnership with the parents and students with whom she works. Mrs. Holden has recently been assigned to work in a classroom of children with autism spectrum disorder (ASD). She knows how much anxiety a new situation can be for students with ASD. Once she gets her class list for the fall, she calls the parents of each of her students and asks if she can come to the home to get to know their child in a familiar setting before the school year starts. She explains that she knows the child may be anxious about starting a new school year in a new classroom with an unfamiliar teacher. Most of the parents are agreeable once she explains the purpose of her visit. One parent, however, seems nervous about having Mrs. Holden come to her home. Mrs. Holden is sensitive and understanding and suggests that they meet in a place that the child likes. When Mrs. Holden meets with each child and his or her parents, she spends time talking with the child and then points out positive attributes she has noted with the parents. She asks the parents about the child's strengths and special interests and what strategies they have found to be effective. She also asks the parents how she can best communicate with them and whether there are specific goals they have for their child.

Because she has established a beginning positive rapport, she asks the parents whether they would like to bring their children to see her classroom before the school year starts without any other children present. She wants to make the transition into her class as positive as possible. All of the parents take her up on her offer; they are eager to see what she will be doing with their children.

SOLUTIONS TO COMMON MISTAKES

Here are some common mistakes that educators make when interacting with parents, followed by an accompanying solution.

Mistake: Becoming defensive when the parents ask a question about why the student is not progressing well

Solution: When parents make a comment because they are concerned about their child, it can be easy to take that comment personally. For instance, the child may be experiencing behavior problems and the parent says, "I do not understand why this is happening; he did not have any problems last year." It would be easy to become defensive and assume that the parents are saying that you are not as good a teacher as the one last year. Active listening, however, serves the teacher best in this situation. Instead of becoming defensive, remember that the parents are concerned, and ask the parents for more information: "Can you tell me more about why you think that?" "What did he like to do last year?"

Mistake: Doing most of the talking in conversations with the parent

Solution: Make sure that conversations with parents encourage and invite the parents to voice their questions and concerns. Ask open-ended questions, actively listen, and reflect statements to ensure that you understand what the parent is saying.

Mistake: Assuming that the teacher knows how best to help the child

Solution: Teachers need to realize that the parent knows the child best. The parent is responsible for the child the majority of the day and sees the child's strengths and weaknesses more than teachers. Teachers are experts in specialized instruction, but parents can provide helpful information when determining what strategies need to be utilized. It is critical to establish a partnership and honor and accept the expertise that parents bring to the table in order to successfully educate all children.

Mistake: Faking an answer to a question

Solution: Parents have access to a wealth of resources and information and may know more than teachers do about a specific strategy. If teachers do not know the answer to a question, then they need to let the parents know that they do not have the answer at this time, but they will be happy to research the answer. Teachers are telling a lie when they fake an answer, which leads to losing the trust of the parents.

Mistake: Failure to introduce yourself to the parents and student in advance of the student coming into your class

Solution: Although teachers may not be able to visit every parent's home, they can at least reach out to parents either via telephone or e-mail before the beginning of the school year, which makes parents feel more comfortable and gives teachers an opportunity to introduce themselves to the parents at the very beginning of the year. It increases teachers' chances of getting off on the right foot.

Mistake: Withholding information from the parents for fear of upsetting them

Solution: Teachers may not want to offend parents, but they should share critical information in a kind and considerate manner instead of withholding it. If teachers have to communicate that the child is having significant behavior problems, then they should do so in a factual and objective manner by sharing data and stressing that they want to work together to better understand the behavior and determine what should be done.

Mistake: Failure to allow enough time at the IEP meeting or during the parent conference to address the parents' concerns

Solution: If teachers have an idea that the parent has concerns, then they should schedule additional time during an IEP meeting or a conference. In general, it is best to allow extra time in case the meeting does not start on schedule because of a conflict. Teachers need to be cautious in scheduling back-to-back meetings because if one parent or a member of the school staff is late, then the whole schedule becomes a problem. It is better to allow too much time than not enough time.

Mistake: Making negative or subjective statements about the student in a home-to-school journal, e-mail, or telephone call

Solution: Comments to parents should be objective and nonjudgmental. It is best to stick to the facts. For example, rather than saying, "Jason did not want to do anything today," say, "Jason struggled to complete his independent math and science tasks. He was able to solve three problems out of 10 in math and answer two of five science questions. I will be working with him to improve his work completion." This information is communicated in an objective manner and is based on facts. It also shows that the teacher will be working with him to improve his work completion. Instead of saying, "Nathan just cannot sit still," say, "Nathan was able to stay in his seat and work 5 out of 15 minutes."

Mistake: Making plans or commitments that are unrealistic

Solution: Teachers need to be realistic before they make a commitment. If they cannot do a journal once a day, then they need to start with a weekly journal or stagger journals for their students. Perhaps do the journal for boys on Monday and girls on Tuesday.

Mistake: Providing written materials to parents that may be difficult to understand

Solution: Review written materials in a conference with the parents whenever possible. That way, teachers can break the material into small parts and explain anything that may be unclear. Teachers can also read the body language of the parents when they are face to face with them. Teachers should reread materials before they send them home to make sure that they are easy to comprehend. Make sure the material is clear and not open to misinterpretation, taking into consideration that parents may read at different levels or that English may not be the primary language at home.

Mistake: Communicating via e-mail when the parent is upset about a situation

Solution: Evans said it well: There is no such thing as "virtual active listening" (2004, p. 6). If a parent is upset, then teachers need to meet face to face so that the written word is not misinterpreted. Teachers need to engage in active listening when a parent is unhappy about something, and that has to be done in person. If teachers have to send an e-mail message, then they need to be cautious about its wording. Teachers need to reread the e-mail several times to make sure that the message is as clear and as positive as possible.

CHAPTER SUMMARY

This chapter stressed parents' critical role in shaping their child's education. Parents bring expert knowledge of their child that can be invaluable to school personnel responsible for ensuring the child reaches his or her potential in school. Parent involvement is not only best practice, but it is also required by law; parents must provide consent and be invited to play a role in the evaluation and placement process for special education services. A collaborative approach is best in meeting the needs of all students. Not only must educators partner with parents, but they must also partner with other school personnel and members of the educational team.

The following chapter discusses **collaboration** between educators, administrators, and **paraprofessionals.**

Chapter 2 Extras and Activities

How to Advise? Tackling the Tough Questions in Special Education

Q: I had an independent evaluation done by a clinical psychologist and a psychiatrist for my 8-year-old son. Both individuals diagnosed my son with ADHD and said I should seek services from the school district. My son is not currently receiving any services from the district. When I shared the evaluations with the school district personnel, they told me that they did not have to do anything about them and they do not have to provide services to him. I paid for the evaluations myself, but should they have a meeting about them? Does my son have any right to services?

A: Although the school district does not have to accept the information in the independent evaluation that you had done at your own expense, it has to recognize the evaluation. As a result, a conference must be convened to review the findings of the evaluation and determine how that evaluation affects the student's education.

Interact

- Interview a teacher who has been frustrated with a parent. Ask the teacher what his or her frustration resulted from and if he or she could have done anything different in hindsight. Were there proactive and positive behaviors that he or she could have exhibited to diffuse the frustration?

- Interview someone who is a parent and have him or her provide his or her top two beliefs about how parents should be treated by the school.

Read and Reflect

- Observe an IEP meeting or think back to an IEP meeting that you participated in and outline five steps that were taken to make the parent feel comfortable in the setting.

- Think about statements that you might use in a conversation with a parent that might be offensive to the parent and could be a barrier to working productively with him or her. For example, "You need to put your child to bed earlier so he will not be so sleepy in the morning."

Online Activities

- *WebQuest:* Review two web sites that are primarily for parents of children with disabilities. What are two ways the site encourages the parent to communicate with school personnel?

- Find a court case that you believe could have been prevented if the school and parent were working cooperatively. Justify your answer.

Two Truths and a Lie*

Read all of these statements. Two are true, and one is a lie. Determine which one is a lie.

1.   If the parents can only come to an IEP meeting on Saturday, then the school must schedule the IEP meeting on Saturday.

2.   Under certain circumstances, the school can hold an IEP meeting if the parent cannot attend.

3.   Parental concerns must be addressed at the IEP meeting.

*Answers for activities noted with an asterisk are provided in the Answer Key for Extras and Activities appendix.

3

The Importance of the Collaborative Team

Partnering with Peers, Administrators, and Paraprofessionals

Communication is a key component for a successful team, especially a team that works with students with disabilities. Educators who are working with students with complex disabilities often face a great deal of stress, which can cause communication to break down. Educators can work well with students and even families but can be so consumed with that important work that they forget to talk with others on the team.

ROLES OF EDUCATIONAL TEAM MEMBERS

Individuals working with students with disabilities work daily with different team members, all of whom have different perspectives. The administrator is responsible for the entire school building and must know when problems arise. He or she is expected to know what is going on within the building and should be kept informed of any changes that may affect the school and its students.

There is a lead teacher responsible for primary supervision of the child, and that individual decides the instructional support that the student needs. He or she must do that in **consultation** with other teachers and related services professionals.

The general education teacher is concerned with all of the students within the classroom and wants to meet their needs. The general education teacher who works with a student with a disability seeks input and guidance from special educators and related services personnel. The general educator also wants other personnel to understand the challenges he or she faces, such as feeling pressure for good test scores and covering the expected curriculum while having large class sizes.

Special education teachers may also be dealing with large caseloads and juggling the demands to provide support for a range of students in a variety of classes. The special educator is expected to provide specialized instruction, make or assist in making accommodations, **co-teach,** direct and supervise paraprofessionals, and collaborate with other members of the IEP team.

A paraprofessional is an individual who provides instructional support for students in a variety of settings. That instructional support is directed by a certified teacher. The role of paraprofessionals in some circumstances, however, has expanded to include activities usually performed by a teacher (Giangreco, Suter, & Hurley, 2011). It is the job of the special educator to provide direction and supervision to the paraprofessional as he or she works with students in the classroom. This relationship can be challenging because the paraprofessional may be older or have more classroom experience than the classroom teacher, so it is important that the two parties work hard to work well together.

Teachers receive training on working with students and their parents, but they are also expected to collaborate with others and supervise paraprofessionals, sometimes without explicit guidance. Some schools have significantly increased the hiring of paraprofessionals rather than employing more special educators or teachers (Giangreco et al., 2011). Teachers find themselves in the position of supervising individuals without receiving any training because of the increase in special education paraprofessionals. The teacher is the primary supervisor for the paraprofessional and must communicate clear expectations for him or her, making it understood that the paraprofessional is provided direction by the teacher rather than acting unilaterally. The paraprofessional is often working with a child with a disability who is in special education and general education, so a lot of physical movement occurs throughout the day in addition to adjusting to changing schedules and courses.

It is critical that the supervising teacher of the paraprofessional frequently observe the work of the paraprofessional in order to determine that the appropriate instructional supports are being provided to individual students, which requires careful attention and close communication. In addition to frequently communicating with the paraprofessional, it also is essential to maintain communication with related services personnel such as SLPs, social workers, school psychologists, and school nurses. These professionals are often faced with large caseloads, providing services to students in more than one building, and collaborating with multiple individuals. The roles of these different professionals are critical to the IEP team, but because each person focuses on a different aspect of support for the student, it is important that every professional clearly communicate with other team members after a careful evaluation of the child. For example, if a student requires specific medical supports, then the school nurse will develop the plan, but he or she may be able to instruct another team member about how to support the student's needs.

It is essential that each individual who is a member of the IEP team understands the viewpoints of others, actively listens to the other team members, and pledges to work together for the common interest of the child. The expertise of each team member is critical to the success of the student, and that expertise needs to be acknowledged and respected. For example, the SLP plays a critical role in a child's education because he or she has been trained to evaluate and design effective methods of communication. The child must be able to communicate his or her needs to students and staff to be successful in school.

BASIC PRINCIPLES OF THE
LAWS AND REGULATIONS REGARDING THE TEAM

IDEA 2004 requires a team approach. The evaluation for students with disabilities is a multidisciplinary one. A group of qualified professionals and the parent of the child determine whether the student is a child with a disability as well as his or her educational needs. Information must be obtained from a variety of sources and must be documented and carefully considered (34 C.F.R. 300.306). The process of creating the IEP requires that a group of individuals come together to communicate their viewpoints and collaborate to meet the needs of the students.

The IEP team also determines placement for the student. Required participants on the team are the parents, not less than one regular education teacher, not less than one special education teacher, a representative of the public agency who may approve services and who is typically the building administrator, "an individual who can interpret the instructional implications of evaluation results, who may also be another member of the team" (20 U.S.C. 1414), and other individuals

Just 3 X 5 It: A Mnemonic to Help You Remember

A successful team approach to working on behalf of students with disabilities is to COLLABORATE.

C—Communication should be kept open and should be frequent.

O—Observe other individuals' needs to see their particular viewpoint.

L—Listen actively to what others are telling you.

L—Learn as much as you can about the role of the other individuals with whom you work.

A—Attend to the needs of others with whom you work.

B—Believe that your colleagues want to work with you, and build on that belief.

O—Opportunities to communicate need to be sought. When are the best times to talk to the administrator, social worker, or speech-language pathologist? Do not wait for the person to come to you. Go to them.

R—Reflect back on what the other team members are saying to you as a way to understand what is being said. Reinforce other individuals when they communicate with you.

A—Accentuate the positive attributes of your colleagues. Just as teachers build on student strengths, they need to also build on their colleagues' strengths. Teachers may be quick to focus on what others are doing wrong, but they should take the time to recognize what people are doing right.

T—Take the time to work with other individuals. Most teachers have a heavy work load and feel their time is limited, but failure to take the time now to work with others may result in loss of time later when communication has broken down.

E—Evaluate your own behavior at all times to determine whether you are putting up roadblocks to communication. Evaluate your role in the problem when you are having problems working with another staff member.

who have knowledge or special expertise regarding the child, and the child, when appropriate (34 C.F.R. 300.321).

All members of the IEP team share the desire to plan an effective educational program for the student. This required team approach is a protection to the student because it ensures that decisions are founded on input from various professionals with diverse knowledge regarding the child's educational needs. Communication is critical to this collaborative approach. This chapter's mnemonic spells out the details of effective collaboration.

Consider the collaborative efforts made in the following How Would You Rule? exercise. Do you think that the team made the best collective decision for the student?

How Would You Rule?

An IEP team decided to place a ninth-grade student with Down syndrome in special education classes for basic academic classes, specifically reading, math, and social studies. The student had spent a great deal of time in her regents-level classes crying and engaging in off-task behavior such as sleeping. Classroom teachers reported that the content of those classes was beyond the comprehension level of the student and the student regressed (Slater, 2014). The IEP team evaluated all aspects of the student's situation and considered each team member's input before making a placement decision.

Was the IEP team's collaborative decision appropriate, or should the student have continued in the general education class?

Your ruling:

_____
_____
_____
_____
_____

The court's ruling:

The court ruled in *V.M. v. North Colonie Central School District* (2013) that the student struggled in her classes, even though she was receiving a significantly modified curriculum and a great deal of individualized instruction that the team was collaboratively planning for her. The IEP team clearly took this decision seriously, and the parent, numerous faculty members, and other support personnel were consulted throughout the process.

CASE STUDY COMPARISON

Compare and contrast how members of the educational team work together in each of these two examples. Communication between team members has broken down in the first example, and there is an unwillingness to collaborate. The second example demonstrates strategies to maintain effective communication, even in the case of a heavy work load or competing responsibilities.

A Case of Missteps and Mistakes

Mrs. Jefferies is a new special education teacher hired to work in an instructional cross-categorical special education classroom. She is looking forward to this assignment and spends time in her classroom well before the school year starts so she can figure out what she is supposed to do. She knows that she will have an instructional aide, Mrs. Holmes, for the entire class. She notices that one of Mrs. Holmes' assignments is to spend two periods a day with three of the special education students in the general education classroom. She is not sure what the responsibilities are for Mrs. Holmes when she is in the general education classroom with the students.

Mrs. Jefferies goes to the classroom teacher with whom Mrs. Holmes worked last year to talk with her about what she did in the classroom. There will be a different general education teacher this year, but she wants to see what Mrs. Holmes previously did to assist the students so she can talk with Mrs. Holmes about her responsibilities for this year. The classroom teacher vents to Mrs. Jefferies that the presence of Mrs. Holmes in her classroom was disruptive because Mrs. Holmes talked loudly, hovered over the special education students, and did most of the work for them. Mrs. Jefferies asks whether she had talked with Mrs. Holmes or the special education teacher about this issue. The classroom teacher said she tried to talk with Mrs. Holmes, who said that she did not have to answer to her. As a result, she talked to the special education teacher, who told her that she could not make Mrs. Holmes change her behavior. The classroom teacher decided to just drop it and became resentful of Mrs. Holmes. She hoped she did not have to take any of Mrs. Jefferies' students again because she did not want anything to do with Mrs. Holmes. Mrs. Jefferies thinks the classroom teacher's position is unreasonable, but she does not say anything to the classroom teacher. Instead, she decides to report the classroom teacher to the building principal. She lets the building principal know that the classroom teacher is unreasonable and asks that he intervene with the teacher. The building principal is upset with Mrs. Jefferies and tells her that she should resolve this problem herself.

What errors were made in this example? Consider the following list of missteps and mistakes:

- The previous special education teacher should have worked with Mrs. Holmes to change her behavior and should have been communicating on a regular basis with the general education teacher.

- The administrator should have been informed by the previous teachers that there was a problem with Mrs. Holmes.

- The district failed to provide training for Mrs. Holmes and quite possibly for the special education teacher regarding supervision.

- Mrs. Jefferies did not see the situation from the classroom teacher's point of view and got upset with her but failed to communicate with her.

- Mrs. Jefferies complained to the building principal before the school year started about a veteran classroom teacher, and the building principal became defensive because Mrs. Jefferies did not try to resolve the issue with the teacher.

How could Mrs. Jefferies have better resolved this situation? Imagine if the following steps were taken:

- Mrs. Jefferies needs to work to build a positive relationship with the new general educator; otherwise the situation is going to snowball because the previous classroom teacher will probably talk with the new classroom teacher and provide her feedback about what happened last year. There will then be problems right from the beginning. Mrs. Jefferies should let the previous teacher know that she is sorry this happened last year and that she wants to prevent a recurrence of this situation, and she should also note that she wants to work with Mrs. Holmes to improve her skills. She should be upfront and tell the new teacher that she plans to meet with the building principal to see what can be done. She might suggest they meet together with the principal to develop a plan.

- Mrs. Jefferies needs to meet with her building principal to discuss the situation with Mrs. Holmes. She gets her building administrator's guidance on what to do and lets her administrator know that she will keep him informed about specific situations. Her building administrator suggests that she meet with Mrs. Holmes and outline her expectations for her. Her administrator also suggests that Mrs. Jefferies, Mrs. Holmes, and the new classroom teacher meet together after that to outline the expectations for Mrs. Holmes. Mrs. Jefferies follows through with these recommendations and reports back to the building principal about progress.

- Mrs. Jefferies could have a meeting with Mrs. Holmes before the school year starts and subsequently plan to meet with her each morning for a few minutes to talk about the expectations for the school day. Mrs. Jefferies models a calm and quiet approach throughout the day. At the end of the day, she checks with the new classroom teacher with whom Mrs. Holmes spends the two periods per day to see how things have gone. The three of them sit down once a week at the end of the day to review the students' progress and to see how Mrs. Jefferies and Mrs. Holmes can better support the classroom teacher. Most days, Mrs. Jefferies and Mrs. Holmes review progress, and Mrs. Jefferies reinforces Mrs. Holmes when she is utilizing a calm approach and providing appropriate support for the students.

The Exemplary Approach

Mr. Hernandez is an SLP who has worked in his school district for more than 10 years. His caseload is 45 students among three buildings, and scheduling his students can be a challenge. He meets with his school administrator and supervisor before school starts to review his caseload and explain how he plans to work together with the teachers. He has learned that it works best to meet either before school starts or at the beginning of the school year with each individual teacher to get his or her schedule and jointly determine the best time to work with the students. He lets the teachers know what days he will be in each building and tells them that they can e-mail or call him if they have questions. Mr. Hernandez provides each teacher with an explanation of the current speech-language levels of the student and the goals he is working to achieve at the first meeting of the school year. He also explains the accommodations that the student may need. He works very hard to accommodate the schedules of the teachers.

He also meets with the special education teachers and other related services personnel who have his students. He stresses how he wants to work closely with each of them, and he gets their input on scheduling. He reminds them that he is only an e-mail, telephone call, or text away.

Mr. Hernandez communicates his completed schedule with the teachers, the administrator and supervisor, and other related services personnel to see if there are any major problems. He makes it a point to check in with the educators who have his students when he is in their building. His goal is to check in with each educator and his administrator at least once a week, and he keeps a log of whom he has talked to, which assists him in monitoring his goal.

Because the administrator knows Mr. Hernandez's schedule and that he is working to frequently communicate, the administrator makes it a point to schedule IEP meetings for Mr. Hernandez's students when he knows Mr. Hernandez will be in the building.

SOLUTIONS TO COMMON MISTAKES

Here are some common mistakes made when working as a team, with suggested ways to repair communication breakdown, better collaborate with colleagues, and fulfill your responsibility as a team member.

Mistake: Not communicating on a regular basis with the building administrator or other supervisor about what is occurring in your classroom or on your caseload

Solution: Administrators like to be kept in the loop of what is happening. They do not like surprises. Educators should be frequently communicating with their administrator or supervisor to let them know what is going on, particularly if there are potentially volatile situations. If personnel have talked with a parent who is upset about services, then the administrator or supervisor needs to be told. If personnel have heard about problems on the bus, then the administrator needs to know. If personnel have observed an instance in which bullying was allowed or have witnessed some other inappropriate handling of a situation, then the administrator or supervisor needs to be immediately notified. Some individuals may perceive that they will be accused of being a tattletale or troublemaker, yet failure to report an incident that was inappropriately handled can result in liability for the witness who did nothing.

I knew a teacher who needed materials for her classroom. She went to local business representatives asking for donations. The principal of the school got a telephone call asking for further information about the needed donations. The principal did not have any idea that donations had been solicited and was upset. Educators need to know their district's policy on donations and make sure they check with the administrator to determine whether solicitation is allowed. This is a good example of the importance of communicating with the building administrator; the teacher should have first verified whether seeking donations was permissible. Many questions come up that are worth running by an administrator. What kinds of videos can be shown in the classroom? What types of activities are allowed? It is important to know school policies and expectations before taking any action.

Mistake: Buying into toxic situations within the school building. A friend of mine who works in a school reported to me that she had allowed herself to get sucked into a volatile situation in the building, and she had been under a great deal of stress as a result.

Solution: Avoid getting sucked in when you find yourself surrounded by colleagues within your building who are continually complaining. Listen empathetically when someone is complaining about a work situation, but do not offer an opinion or start complaining. Attempt to change the conversation to something positive when you are in a group that tends to make a lot of negative comments. If you find yourself in these situations and you cannot change others' behavior, then identify that you are in a toxic situation and avoid the group. Otherwise, you bring yourself down. I knew a teacher who was in such a situation and she would say, "I close my classroom door and just stay in my classroom." Avoid situations when individuals are complaining about students. You may find yourself quoted by others, and information can get back to other staff and families.

Mistake: Allowing others to tell you what to do when what they are telling you to do is not in the best interest of the student and may violate the student's IEP

Solution: Always put the needs of the students above everything. Having been involved in thousands of IEPs during my career, I have received a great deal of pressure to recommend placements that I did not believe were appropriate for students and make decisions that violated the **continuum of alternative placements.** I learned that I had to stick with my convictions about what the individual child needed, even though it sometimes came at a great personal cost. Superintendents would try to threaten my job, and some other individuals would ostracize me, but I could look in the mirror at the end of the day and know that I had done what was in the best interests of the student. It was interesting that when I would speak up on behalf of the child, having done my homework so that I could justify what I recommended, it gave others the courage to do the same.

I can remember one instance in which a superintendent tried to pressure me into putting a student in a self-contained separate setting when the child had not even been given the opportunity to be in an LRE. When I spoke up and talked about the need for another placement option, stating that I would complete a minority report because I did not agree with the placement recommendation, several other members of the team spoke up as well with the same viewpoint. The minority became the majority, and an LRE was recommended for the child.

Mistake: Failure to monitor the work of other individuals who are under your supervision

Solution: If you are responsible for supervising other professionals, then observe their work. If you are a special educator, then it is your responsibility to supervise the paraprofessionals that are assigned to you. This can be difficult, particularly if the paraprofessional does not want to take direction or has strong ideas about how to work with the student, as can happen in any working relationship. If you are a young, new teacher, then you might end up supervising an older paraprofessional, which may feel unnatural because of the age difference. You must closely monitor the paraprofessional's work with students, regardless, because you are ultimately responsible if anything goes wrong. Special educators often get busy with all the other responsibilities they have and may be tempted to take the easy path of just letting the paraprofessional do what he or she thinks is best for the student; however, what the paraprofessional thinks is best may not be in accordance with the student's IEP, which must be followed.

An integral part of the monitoring process is regularly scheduled meetings with the individuals you are responsible for supervising. You must provide constructive feedback as part of the supervision process and let the individual know what he or she is doing right and what needs to be changed or improved. Some educators meet twice daily with their paraprofessionals, once in the morning to review what the plans are for the day and again at the end of the day to review what happened well and what needs to be changed for the next day. It is advisable to follow up with the recommendations in writing when there are trouble areas and certain changes need to be made to someone's work. You are creating a paper trail and proof that you have made specific recommendations.

A debriefing at the end of each day with the social worker and the principal was one of the most beneficial activities that occurred for me as a new teacher. I could review what had happened that day and what needed to be changed. Then we could all talk about constructive activities for the next day. I knew I had support, which was critical to my success as a brand new teacher.

Mistake: Allowing others under your supervision to engage in tasks that are beyond their range of responsibility and training

Solution: A major problem in schools today is that paraprofessionals are being hired at a greater rate than professionals are being employed (Johns, 2014; Richmond, 2014). Paraprofessionals may be engaging in activities that are beyond their training. Paraprofessionals should support instruction that is clearly planned by the professional educator. They do not plan the instruction for the students. Educators have a major responsibility to make sure that they are planning the instruction for the student. The paraprofessional is to be supervised by the professional and works under the direction of the professional. Paraprofessionals should be provided with a clear assignment of what they are expected to do and an understanding of what they are not expected to do before they are employed.

Mistake: Failure to document when you have requested that other staff members do something for one of your students that is required by the IEP

Solution: If you are working with a colleague who is not fulfilling his or her responsibilities as delineated in the IEP, then it is critical that you discuss the issue with the individual and then document the conversation in writing. Perhaps a related services provider is supposed to be seeing a student for 30 minutes a week. Five weeks into the beginning of the school year, the student is not being seen. You have a responsibility to follow up and discuss your observations and the rationale for why the student is not being seen. You must then document the conversation; otherwise, the individual may claim to not know that he or she was supposed to be seeing the student.

CHAPTER SUMMARY

Team members must regularly coordinate, communicate, and collaborate as mandated by IDEA 2004 to ensure the child gets every educational need met. It is sometimes necessary to supervise other members on the team, which can come with challenges. Interpersonal difficulties, stress, time constraints, and strong beliefs about what is best for the child are other barriers to effective teamwork; yet, many strategies and solutions can help bolster the partnerships among school personnel. Effective listening, respect for each team member's discipline-specific expertise, and a shared vision or goal for helping the student succeed can all be instrumental in strengthening the teamwork required for evaluating the child for special education, developing the IEP, and determining placement. The IEP is the focus of the following chapter, which details important legal responsibilities and considerations related to this essential document.

Chapter 3 Extras and Activities

How to Advise? Tackling the Tough Questions in Special Education Law

Q: My 10-year-old child has autism and is in a special education resource class for 2 hours per day and in a general education fourth-grade classroom for the remainder of the day. It was determined as a part of his IEP that he would have a one-to-one assistant. He has a new one-to-one assistant this year, and it seems like he is regressing. He seems to be more dependent on the assistant, and when I have asked the special education teacher and the general education teacher how they think he is doing, they do not seem to know much about his progress and refer me to the one-to-one assistant. It appears to me that the assistant is providing most of his instruction. What are the responsibilities of the general and special education teachers?

A: The general and special education teachers ultimately should be designing and delivering instruction as specified by the IEP. You have several options as a parent because you have attempted to work with the general and special education teachers. You can schedule an appointment with the building principal or the supervisor of special education to discuss the problem. Or, you can specifically ask for a new IEP team meeting for your child and explain your concerns at the team meeting.

Interact

- Interview an individual who serves in a different role than you. Ask that individual to list five communication barriers in the IEP team meeting that he or she sees from his or her perspective.

- Get into groups of five to six people. Group members in an in-service session can be assigned to a role that they do not have in the real world—administrator, classroom teacher, special education teacher, and paraprofessional—and then give their insight into the solutions to this chapter's missteps and mistakes from the viewpoint of the position that they are role playing. Individuals in a preservice session can draw from a hat or a bag the role they will play.

- Divide into two different groups. If the group is large, then choose five individuals for each side—one in favor of the question and one opposed. Then debate this issue: "Should paraprofessionals be able to deliver instruction?" One group opposes paraprofessionals delivering instruction, and one group favors paraprofessionals delivering instruction.

Online Activities

- *WebQuest:* Review the web sites of three different professional organizations representing three different disciplines (e.g., school psychologists, SLPs, general education teachers, secondary or elementary principals, special education teachers). Summarize the three key issues that you learned about from those web sites. How are the three organizations different? What are three similar issues they are facing?

- Find an article that was written for paraprofessionals, and summarize three different points from that article.

Two Truths and a Lie*

Read all of these statements. Two are true, and one is a lie. Determine which one is a lie.

1. The special education teacher's opinion weighs the heaviest on the IEP team because the special educator has expertise in the IEP.

2. The paraprofessional is not responsible for planning instruction for the student.

3. There must be an administrator on every IEP team who is able to approve services.

*Answers for activities noted with an asterisk are provided in the Answer Key for Extras and Activities appendix.

4

Basic Principles
of the IEP

The IEP is at the heart of special education because it is the driving force in documenting what is appropriate for students with disabilities. The Education for All Handicapped Children Act of 1975 (PL 94-142) recognized that each student in special education is different and a yearly educational plan should be developed by a team of individuals. That IEP remains central in educating students with disabilities. A multidisciplinary team of school personnel comes together with the parents and the child at least once a year to review information about the child and determine his or her individual needs. The team specifically reviews the student's present levels of academic achievement and functional performance, determines the student's needs, and then decides how to meet those needs by setting goals and objectives that will be implemented for the year. The team designs instruction and support after the goals are determined to assist the student in achieving those goals.

IEP VERSUS INDIVIDUAL 504 PLAN

A child with a disability is not necessarily eligible for special education services (see Chapter 1). There are students with disabilities who are not in special education because their disability does not have an adverse impact on educational performance. Students who qualify for an IEP are those who have been diagnosed with a disability from one of the categories listed in IDEA 2004—intellectual disabilities; hearing impairments, including deafness; speech-language impairments; visual impairments, including blindness; emotional disturbance; orthopedic impairments; autism; traumatic brain injury; other health impairments; specific learning disabilities; multiple disabilities; and deaf-blindness (34 C.F.R. 300.8). This disability must affect the student's educational performance such that he or she requires special education and related services. There are other students with disabilities that require accommodations delineated in a Section 504 plan, but they do not need special education.

How does the IEP differ from the individual 504 plan? Accommodation plans are developed for students who require supports that provide them with comparable services to other students. IEPs are based on individual educational needs, should incorporate accommodations for students, and determine how to meet the student's differing learning needs. A student with diabetes is an example of someone who may need a 504 plan and not special education. The student has a disability, but the disability does not affect educational performance, so he or she does not need special education. The student still can achieve at grade level without specialized supports related to academics, but he or she does need certain accommodations. The 504 plan might include more frequent restroom breaks, a water bottle, and the need to go to the school nurse to monitor blood sugar. If this same student also had a learning disability or was considered as having a health impairment (one of the disability categories designated in IDEA 2004) because the disability had an adverse impact on educational performance, then an IEP would be developed to meet his or her needs for special education and would also include the accommodations for the diabetes.

The IEP outlines the specially designed instruction that is needed to ensure a student makes meaningful progress toward his or her educational goals. It may be that the student needs a multisensory approach to reading instruction, which might mean that the student will be provided with a print out of lecture notes or will be taught specific memory techniques. Regardless, the instruction and supports are specifically designed for that individual and are based on a thorough assessment of the student's needs.

Specially designed instruction should involve intensive interventions that are data based. The special educator provides an individualized intervention that is based on the student's needs. Data is collected while the intervention is being delivered to ensure that the intervention is effective. If not, then the special educator either increases the intensity of the intervention or changes the intervention and continues to collect data on effectiveness.

THE IEP MEETING

The IEP process begins with an evaluation of the child and an initial meeting to determine eligibility for special education services. The results of the evaluation are documented in an IEP eligibility meeting and utilized to determine eligibility. IDEA 2004 allows for the consolidation of IEP team meetings. For example, the IEP team can have an eligibility meeting and then move right into the placement meeting at the same scheduled time, provided they have furnished **prior written notice** to the parent in writing of the purpose of the meeting. The team must consider a continuum of alternative placements when deciding where the child should be placed. By law, the continuum of alternative placements available should include, but is not limited to, instruction in the general education classroom, special classrooms, or special schools; instruction in the home; or instruction in hospitals or other institutional settings, with the goal to place the student in the LRE possible for him or her to succeed (Pennsylvania State Education Association, 2015). IEP meetings are held after eligibility and placement are determined to create and discuss the IEP. In addition to the required yearly IEP meetings, the child must be reevaluated every 3 years. The schools must encourage the consolidation of reevaluation meetings for the child and other IEP team meetings for the child to the greatest extent possible (34 C.F.R. 300.324).

School personnel are allowed to come to the IEP meeting with a draft of the IEP document for review by the parent and other school personnel, but it should always be clear to the parent that this is only a draft and that the document is subject to change. Having a draft of the IEP allows for active notetaking and serves as a concrete reminder of what the current IEP states. Best practice would say that if a draft is going to be discussed, then the draft should be sent to the parents in advance so they can review it to determine changes they would like to see made and also to prepare any questions they may have. See Figure 4.1 for a checklist of suggestions and reminders for IEP meeting participants as they prepare for the meeting.

During the IEP meeting, numerous staff members, service providers, and family members will be discussing what supports and interventions are most appropriate for a student. The IEP process can often be overwhelming to the parent, so it is important to be prepared and speak slowly and carefully. Educators should consider their word choice while talking at the IEP meeting to make sure that they are not utilizing jargon that may be unfamiliar to the parent or others in the meeting.

Parental input is continually sought throughout the process. Parents should be provided the opportunity to share their concerns and ask questions without feeling that they will be criticized; their thoughts and opinions must be valued and appreciated. Educators and other team members have to remember that the parents know the child better than anyone else. Parents are excellent resources in knowing their child's strengths, weaknesses, and interests, and that information is important in the IEP process—the team should work on remediating weaknesses while

---

A Checklist for Individualized Education Program (IEP) Team Members to Prepare for an IEP

Have I reviewed the records of the student so that I have an understanding of the child's background and the child's needs?

Am I keeping data on the student's academic and behavioral progress within my area of expertise, and am I prepared to share that information?

Am I prepared to make statements in both the academic and functional performance section that are written in measurable, observable, and objective terms?

Can a stranger understand what the needs of the student are based on what I have communicated?

Am I prepared with suggested goals and, where appropriate, objectives for the student?

Have I written down information about what accommodations I have used and which ones have been effective or ineffective?

Am I prepared to provide constructive feedback about the needs of the student and how the student is succeeding compared with peers?

Am I prepared to frame weaknesses into factual information?

Am I prepared to contribute constructive comments about what supports the student needs to be successful?

Am I prepared to ask questions to clarify any statements made by parents or other colleagues? If I do not agree with a statement, I will state so, along with the reason I do not agree.

Figure 4.1. Checklist to prepare for the individualized education program.

capitalizing on strengths and interests when creating an IEP. Parents also have ideas about what specific goals on which they would like to see school personnel work. A productive working relationship can be established with the parents when the IEP is viewed as a collaborative document.

If there is someone recording information discussed during the IEP meeting, then consider having the parent sit next to that person. This allows the parent to see what actually is being written or typed. You may also project what is being typed onto a large screen so that all participants can view notes from the meeting. That allows everyone to proofread what is being typed to make sure that what is recorded is what is actually being said.

All IEP team members must work hard to establish a comfortable environment for parents when they attend the IEP meeting. Little things such as providing a cup of coffee or some water can go a long way to making parents feel welcome. It is important that all meeting participants are on time and prepared for the meeting because showing up late or unprepared suggests a lack of respect for others' time, particularly for the student and his or her family. Remember these 10 welcoming tips when holding an IEP meeting:

1. Be on time.

2. Explain the process and the purpose of the meeting.

3. Make sure participants briefly describe their role in the process when they introduce themselves.

4. Offer refreshments.

5. Refrain from using jargon.

6. Provide objective information rather than giving subjective opinions.

7. Provide positive information and factual information concerning the weaknesses of the student.

8. Ask parents for their input throughout the process.

9. Engage in active listening.

10. Avoid sidebar conversations. The parents are trying to process a lot of oral information and may be easily distracted by sidebar conversations.

Following a successful IEP meeting, participants will have contributed thoughts and facts to shape individualized, meaningful goals and objectives for a student; consensus will have been reached among all participants; and a comprehensive, meaningful IEP will have been written. The time spent in these meetings is of the utmost importance because the IEP is a document that affects the child's life and paves the way for the child's educational future. All team members come to the table to develop a plan that will meet the needs of the child.

BASICS OF THE LAWS AND REGULATIONS REGARDING THE IEP

The IEP is an agreement between school district personnel and the parents and student about what the child needs, how the services will be delivered, and by whom. The first question I raise when someone says that he or she thinks the student no longer needs speech-language therapy or he or she believes the student needs more time in special education is: "What does the current IEP say?"

The IEP document should be front and center in any discussion about an individual child. Whether discussing testing accommodations, number of minutes in speech-language therapy, or appropriate **positive behavior interventions and supports (PBIS)**, the IEP must be reviewed, and the team should reconvene if the document does not reflect the child's needs.

The law and regulations of the IEP can be broken down into the "who" of the IEP—who participates; the "what" of the IEP—the content; the "when" of the IEP—important time lines; and the "how" of the IEP—the IEP process.

Who Participates in Developing and Implementing the IEP?

The IEP is the driving force in planning instruction for the student who is receiving special education and is created by a multidisciplinary group of individuals who make up the IEP team. Legally mandated participants include the parents of the child; at least one of the student's general education teachers; at least one of the student's special education teachers or service providers; the building administrator or special education coordinator who supervises programs and understands the availability of resources in the building; someone who can interpret the instructional implications of evaluation results and may be one of the other members of the team, such as the special educator, school psychologist, or diagnostician; other individuals who, at the discretion of the parent or agency, have knowledge or special expertise regarding the child, including related services personnel, a coach, or other school staff; and the child with a disability (34 C.F.R. 300.321).

The school district must invite the child with a disability to attend the IEP meeting if the meeting is to consider postsecondary goals for the child and the **transition services** needed to assist the child in reaching those goals (34 C.F.R. 300.321). If the child does not attend the IEP team meeting, then the public agency (e.g., department of vocational rehabilitation, department of developmental disabilities) must take other steps to ensure that the child's preferences and interests are considered (34 C.F.R. 300.321). When conducting a transition plan, the school "must invite a child with a disability to attend his or her IEP if a purpose of the meeting will be the consideration of the post-secondary goals for the child and the transition services needed" (34 C.F.R. 300.321).

The IEP team expands to include **transition services participants**. "To the extent appropriate, with the consent of the parents or a child who has reached the age of majority, the public agency must invite a representative of any participating agency that is likely to be responsible for providing or paying for transition services" (34 C.F.R. 300.321).

The school must invite a representative of any participating agency that is likely to be responsible for providing or paying for transition services to the extent appropriate with the consent of the parents or a child who has reached the age of majority (34 C.F.R. 300.321). These agencies might also include the department of social services, local chamber of commerce, or local mental health agency, if the student has mental health needs. If the student has been involved in the foster care system, then the Department of Children and Family Services may be involved.

There may also be a youth center in the community with which the student has been involved.

What if someone cannot attend the IEP? IEP team members may be excused from all or part of the meeting if the parent of the student and the school agree in writing that the attendance of the member is not necessary. For example, the SLP is unable to be present, and there are no proposed changes to the student's speech-language supports. The parent may give written permission for the SLP to be excused from the meeting. The SLP then provides a written report to be included with the IEP. For example, the student is in multiple general education classes at the secondary level. One teacher is present, but another teacher is not able to attend. That individual is excused from the meeting and then submits a report with details about the student's performance in class, along with any other relevant information for the IEP team.

The parent is an integral part of the IEP process. Schools must take steps to ensure that one or both of the parents of a child with a disability are present at each IEP team meeting or are afforded the opportunity to participate. Parents should be notified about the meeting far enough in advance so that they can make plans to attend, and the meeting should occur at a mutually agreed-on time and place. An IEP team meeting may be conducted without a parent in attendance if the school is unable to convince the parent that he or she should attend. If this is the case, then the school must keep a record of its attempts to arrange a mutually agreed-on time and place, such as detailed records of telephone calls made or attempted and the results of those calls, copies of correspondence sent to the parents and any responses received, and detailed records of visits made to the parents' home or place of employment and the results of those visits (34 C.F.R. 300.321).

If the parent needs an interpreter in order to understand the proceedings of the IEP team meeting, then the school must take whatever action is necessary to arrange for an interpreter for a parent who is deaf or whose native language is other than English. It is critical that schools know the licensing requirements for interpreters in their own state (34 C.F.R. 300.322). For example, if a school needs to employ an interpreter for American Sign Language, then there are states that require that the individual has a specific license to interpret within the schools.

What Is Involved in the IEP Process?

The IEP team must consider the strengths of the child; the concerns of the parents for enhancing their child's education; the results of the most recent evaluation of the child; and the "academic, developmental, and functional needs of the child" (34 C.F.R. 300.324). The team looks at all the information they have about the evaluation and the student's current academic achievement levels and functional levels. The team then writes goals and objectives based on that information. The district then determines how and where to meet the needs of the student. An overview of the IEP sequence is provided in Figure 4.2.

It is critical that all members of the IEP team receive training on the importance of their role in writing IEPs. Training for individual members of the team should include instruction on

- Understanding the required components of the IEP

- Giving proper written notice and how to provide proper notice

The student—background, instructional implications of evaluation, strengths, parent concerns

Present levels of academic achievement and functional performance

Goals and, where appropriate, objectives

Where and how can the goals be met? What specially designed instruction will occur?
Placement, related services, special considerations, assessment plans

Figure 4.2.   The individualized education program (IEP) sequence.

- Identifying the strengths of the student

- Writing academic performance and functional levels in measurable, observable, and objective (MOO) terms

- Writing meaningful goals and objectives

- Creating an effective BIP

- Understanding the requirements of the LRE and the need for a continuum of alternative placements

- Determining the supports for the student and staff

A number of excellent resources for writing effective IEPs can be used for staff development (Bateman & Herr, 2006; Winterman & Rosas, 2014).

Special factors related to the individual child must be considered on a case-by-case basis during the IEP process. A number of key considerations are required by law when developing, implementing, and revising the IEP. The team must consider using PBIS or other evidence-based behavioral strategies in the case of a child whose behavior impedes his or her learning or that of others. They must consider the language needs of the child with limited English proficiency as those needs relate to the child's IEP. The team must provide for instruction in braille and the use of braille for a child who is blind or visually impaired, unless the team determines that braille is not necessary for the student. The IEP team must also consider the communication needs of the child. In the case of a child who is deaf or hard of hearing, the team must specifically "consider the child's language and communication needs, opportunities for direct communication with peers and professional personnel in the child's language and communication mode, academic level, and full range of needs, including opportunities for direct instruction in the child's language and communication mode..." (34 C.F.R. 300.324). The need for **assistive technology (AT) services or devices** is another critical consideration for all students in special education. This includes an evaluation to determine the specific services that are needed.

Travel training may be required as an integral part of the IEP for some students. **Travel training** is defined as "Instruction, as appropriate, to children with significant intellectual disabilities and any other children with disabilities who require this instruction to enable them to (i) Develop an awareness of the environment in which they live; and (ii) Learn the skills necessary to move effectively and safely from place to place within that environment; e.g., in school, in the home, at work, and in the community" (34 C.F.R. 300.39).

The classroom teacher is a required member of the IEP team and must participate in the development of the IEP, including the development of instructional goals and objectives. The classroom teacher also has a role in determining appropriate PBIS and other strategies for the child, including **supplementary aids and services,** program modification, and support for school personnel (34 C.F.R. 300.324). Once goals and objectives are written, the team determines how the student will reach his or her educational outcomes and what instruction and supports the student will need to meet the goals. The classroom teacher is the provider of the general curriculum and brings important knowledge about what outcomes are required for the student at a specific grade level. The classroom teacher should play an active role in these specific IEP team activities and should come prepared to the IEP meeting with the following information:

- The student's present levels of academic achievement and functional performance in the classroom

- Recommended goals and objectives for the student

- Recommended PBIS

- The supplementary aids that are needed for the student (e.g., accommodations, **modifications,** specialized equipment or learning materials)

- Accommodations and/or modifications that are needed for the student to succeed

- Any supports that the teacher needs to successfully work with the student

The IEP document must contain a statement of the child's present levels of academic achievement and functional performance, including how the child's disability affects his or her involvement and progress in the general curriculum. In the case of a preschooler, the team must address how the disability affects the child's participation in appropriate activities. The IEP then includes a statement of measurable annual goals, including academic and functional goals designed to meet the child's needs that result from his or her disability. The IEP must also include statements of how the team will enable the child to be involved and make progress in the general education curriculum and meet each of the child's other educational needs that result from his or her disability. A description of benchmarks or short-term objectives also needs to be included for students who take alternate assessments aligned to alternate academic achievement standards. You should make sure you know the specific laws and regulations in your state because some states require objectives for all children in special education. There must also be a description of how the child's progress toward meeting the annual goals will be measured and when periodic progress reports, concurrent with the issuance of report cards, will be provided (34 C.F.R. 300.320).

The team develops a statement of special education and related services, as well as supplementary aids and services that must be provided to the child, based on the goals and objectives written in the IEP. The type of instruction provided to the child should be based on peer-reviewed research. A statement of program modifications or supports for school personnel might be required in implementing the IEP, including professional development or training for staff, inclusion of an aide or other professional in the classroom, or special equipment or teaching materials (Center for Parent Information and Resources, 2010). An explanation of the extent, if any, to which the child will not participate with typically developing children in the general education class must also be included in the IEP. For example, the child may need more intensive, specially designed one-to-one instruction for a period of time, or the student may have such intense behavioral needs that the classroom teacher is unable to meet those needs in a large-group setting. There is also a statement of any individual appropriate accommodations that are necessary to measure the academic achievement and functional performance of the child on state and districtwide assessments. If the IEP team determines that the child must take an alternate assessment, then they must provide a reason why the child cannot participate in the regular assessment and why the particular alternate assessment is appropriate for the child. Finally, the team must also document the projected date for the beginning of the special education services and modifications and the anticipated frequency, location, and duration of the services (34 C.F.R. 300.320).

The IEP must include transition services, including measurable postsecondary goals and the courses of study needed to achieve the goals, when the child turns 16 years of age, or younger if determined by the team (34 C.F.R. 300.320). Beginning not later than 1 year before the child reaches the age of majority under state law, the IEP has to include a statement that the child has been informed of his or her rights and that **transfer of rights at the age of majority** will take place. (34 C.F.R. 300.320).

In the case of children who attend a private school as a result of parent choice, there must be a statement of the specific services that will be provided to the child with a disability in order to receive special education and related services. The school district must develop a service plan that includes services that would be based on the proportionate share that the district receives from the federal government for the student (34 C.F.R. 300.132 and 300.133).

Important IEP Time Lines

A meeting to develop an IEP for a child is conducted within 30 days of determining that the child needs special education and related services (34 C.F.R. 300.323). The IEP must be reviewed yearly to ensure that meaningful goals and reasonable supports are included. Each school must have an updated IEP for each child with a disability within its jurisdiction at the beginning of each school year (34 C.F.R. 300.320). Evaluations must be conducted every 3 years, and a new IEP is also developed during that time.

IEP team meetings can also be called more than once a year. Some IEP teams determine that they will meet once a quarter or once a semester because of the intensity of the student's needs. The frequency depends on the needs of the child and also on the requests of the parents and individual team members. The parent or a teacher may determine that he or she has concerns about the child's progress.

It is advisable to meet together to review the IEP more often than once a year when that occurs.

The How of the IEP

The IEP process involves many "hows." How do we ensure parent participation in the IEP? How do we implement an IEP for a child who has moved into our school district? How do we transmit the IEP when a child moves? How is an IEP implemented when a parent does not agree? How do we make changes to the IEP without having a new IEP meeting? Each of these important, frequently asked questions will be addressed individually in this section.

How Do We Ensure Parent Participation in the IEP?   If neither parent is able to attend the IEP, then the school must use other methods to ensure parent participation, including individual or conference telephone calls (34 C.F.R. 300.322). The parents of a child with a disability and the school may agree to use **alternative means of meeting participation,** such as video conferences and conference calls (34 C.F.R. 300.328).

How Do We Implement an IEP for a Child Who Has Moved into Our School District?   If a student moves from one district to another within the state and enrolls in a new school, then the new school, in consultation with the parents, must provide the child with a FAPE based on the previous IEP until the new school either adopts the child's IEP from the previous school or develops, adopts, and implements a new IEP. If a student moves from one state to another, then the new school must provide the child a FAPE, including services from the previous IEP, until a new evaluation is conducted and a new IEP is developed and implemented (34 C.F.R. 300.323).

How Do We Transmit the IEP When a Child Moves?   The new school must take reasonable steps to promptly obtain the child's records, including the IEP and supporting documents and any other records relating to the provision of special education or related services. The previous school district in which the child was enrolled must take reasonable steps to promptly respond to the request from the new public agency (34 C.F.R. 300.323).

How Is an IEP Implemented When a Parent Does Not Agree?   Services cannot be initiated if a parent does not agree to his or her child being placed in special education or related services. A school district that is responsible for making a FAPE available to a child with a disability must obtain informed consent from the parent of the child before the initial provision of special education and related services, and the school district must make reasonable efforts to obtain informed consent from the parent. If the parent of a child fails to respond or refuses to consent to services, then the public school may not use due process procedures to obtain agreement or a ruling that the services may be provided to the child. If the parent of the child refuses to consent to the initial provision of special education and related services, then the school will not be considered to be in violation of the requirements to make a FAPE available to the child, and the public agency is not required to convene an IEP team meeting or develop an IEP (34 C.F.R. 300.300). The school cannot use a parent's refusal to consent to one service or activity to deny the parent or child any other service, benefit, or activity of the school.

How Do We Make Changes to the IEP without Having a New Meeting?

The parent of a child with a disability and the public agency may agree not to convene an IEP team meeting for the purposes of making changes to the IEP after the annual IEP meeting and instead may develop a written document to amend or modify the child's current IEP. The school district must ensure that the child's IEP team is informed of those changes. Changes to the IEP may be made either by the entire IEP team at an IEP team meeting or by amending the IEP, rather than by redrafting the entire IEP. Upon request, the parent must be provided with a revised copy of the IEP with the amendments incorporated (34 C.F.R. 300.324).

This chapter's mnemonic helps readers to remember the key points in developing and implementing an IEP.

Considering the student's unique needs and individualizing the goals for the student is of paramount importance when developing the IEP. The following How Would You Rule? exercise invites you to critically think about how you might develop, individualize, and prioritize IEP goals for an actual student.

Just 3 X 5 It: A Mnemonic to Help You Remember

The INDIVIDUAL needs of the student must be the focus when developing the individualized education program (IEP).

I—Individualized for the child

N—Needs of the individual student and concerns of the parents are addressed

D—Developed by a team of individuals who are knowledgeable about the needs of the child

I—Instructional goals are written based on the present levels of academic achievement and functional performance of the student

V—Value the input of parents and all other team members

I—Independent evaluations are considered as part of the process

D—Decisions are made by the multidisciplinary IEP team

U—Unique to the needs of the particular child; no two IEPs are alike

A—Appropriate for the needs of the student and completed annually; decisions are based on what is appropriate for the child, not what is available

L—Least restrictive environment based on the needs of the child; placement is determined from a continuum of alternative placements

How Would You Rule?

The IEP of a ninth-grade student contained a reading goal for the student that was based on the ninth-grade state standards. The student was reading at a first-grade level. The student was going to participate in a specific assessment program to improve his reading competency. The district developed a transition plan that called for the student to improve communication skills, and he would participate in a note-taking class available to all freshman students to meet that goal. Should the student's goals be based on the ninth-grade standards or on this student's need for increasing his reading skills beyond a first-grade level? Was the transition plan developed adequate for the student?

Your ruling:

_____

_____

_____

_____

The court's ruling:

It was determined in *Jefferson County Board of Education v. Lolita S.* (11th circuit, 2014) that the student's IEP goals were not adapted to meet the needs of the student. The goals were not designed for his reading skills and transition needs. There was not any evidence that the student had increased his reading skills from the first-grade level to the ninth-grade level, and a program was not provided to the student to address the gap between the ninth-grade level goal and the first-grade reading level. Although the student was going to participate in a specific reading assessment program, it was determined that this was actually an assessment and not a substantive program to improve reading competency. The IEP was not reasonably calculated to enable the student to receive educational benefit. Another student's name was on some of the pages, which suggested that the district was utilizing stock goals for students rather than using individualized goals. The district failed to conduct a transition assessment prior to developing the goal for transition, and the note-taking class that the student was going to take was open to all freshmen in the school and was therefore not individualized for this student.

CASE STUDY COMPARISON

The following case studies present an educational team in charge of developing and implementing an IEP for a student with disabilities. A serious lack of communication occurs between team members in the first example, causing the student to miss out on needed services. The team in the exemplary approach coordinates and collaborates to develop a comprehensive educational plan for the student.

A Case of Missteps and Mistakes

Brenton is a sixth-grade student with autism who receives special education for 2 hours a day, and he is in a general education class for the remainder of the day. Brenton's mother is upset because she thought Brenton was supposed to receive occupational therapy for 40 minutes per week, and he was supposed to have a one-to-one parapro-fessional. His last IEP was held in January 2014, and it is now October 2014. Brenton's mother has a conference with his special education teacher and voices her concerns about the lack of occupational therapy and the one-to-one paraprofessional. The special education teacher says that Brenton's IEP will be due in January 2015, and they can see about occupational therapy and the paraprofessional at that time. Brenton's mother is not happy and goes to the building principal, who agrees with the teacher and says they will have an IEP meeting in January. In the meantime, he will check the IEP to see what it says about occupational therapy.

The principal checks the IEP and sees that Brenton is supposed to have occupa-tional therapy for 40 minutes per week, but there is nothing noted about a one-to-one paraprofessional. The principal checks with the occupational therapist, who reports that she was not at the last meeting because she did not know about it. She reports that she had previously seen Brenton for several years but assumed that occupational therapy had been dropped. The principal did not participate in the previous IEP because he is new to the district, so he does not know what happened. He checks with the special education teacher, who reports that Brenton had a paraprofessional assigned to him in the past. The team discussed a paraprofessional and believed Brenton needed one, but the previous principal reported that it would not be possible to fund a paraprofessional to support Brenton due to budget cuts. As a result, it was not written on the IEP. The mother files for a due process hearing over the lack of services.

What errors were made in this example? Consider the following lists of missteps and mistakes:

- The district has significant problems. It did not follow what was written in the IEP about Brenton needing occupational therapy services. The occupational therapist was not invited to the last IEP meeting, and the designated case man-ager, who was the special education teacher, should have followed up with the occupational therapist to see that she received a copy of the IEP and knew that occupational therapy was recommended.

- The IEP team should have come to closure on the issue of the paraprofessional before leaving the meeting.

- The team should have suggested reconvening the IEP team to address the mother's concerns rather than waiting until the annual meeting.

What should the new principal, special education teacher, and occupational thera-pist have done, and how can they prevent this from reoccurring?

- The occupational therapist should have been invited to the IEP meeting, and she should have been asked to submit a report if she could not attend. The oc-cupational therapist also had a responsibility to check about whether she was to continue occupational therapy services rather than assuming that occupa-tional therapy had been discontinued.

- There should have been further discussion about the paraprofessional, and a decision should have been made about whether the child would have a paraprofessional's support. Although the principal approves services, it was questionable whether he could override the decision of the group because of financial reasons when the student had a paraprofessional before. One of the ways this could have been handled was to have an IEP meeting prior to the beginning of the school year to determine whether the financial picture of the district had changed. Discussion should have occurred about the rationale for a paraprofessional, and then a determination should have been made.

- The team should have looked into reconvening the IEP team earlier or amending the document as soon as possible rather than strictly adhering to the annual schedule. This would have helped to ensure that Brenton's needs were addressed in a timely manner and that parental concerns were alleviated, which may have helped to avoid a due process hearing.

The Exemplary Approach

Mrs. Walker, the SLP for Jackson, works closely with Mrs. Hamm, the resource special education teacher who sees Jackson for two periods per day. They have noticed during the last 9 weeks that Jackson, a third grader, is not progressing with his speech and language and that he is reading at a mid–first-grade level. Mrs. Walker and Mrs. Hamm confer with the classroom teacher, Mrs. Corell, who shares her belief that Jackson is regressing, but she cannot figure out why this is happening. The three of them meet with the building principal, who suggests that they contact the parent for a parent conference. They do so, and Jackson's mom shares her concern that Jackson may need more special education services. They all agree that an IEP team meeting should be reconvened to determine what services would be more appropriate for Jackson to help him achieve his goals.

After the parent conference is over, the SLP and the special education teacher work together to write up the parent conference, share it with the principal, and place it in the file. They discuss the need for a new IEP meeting with the principal, and he agrees to schedule the meeting. He checks with his staff to determine when they are available. He then calls the parent and sets up a **mutually agreeable time** within the next 10 days. He asks his secretary to get the notice out, and he also sends a reminder about the meeting. The principal chairs the IEP meeting and introduces all of the participants and states their roles. He talks about the rules for the meeting and asks that all participants refrain from any sidebar conversations. He lets the parent know that any time she has questions, she should feel free to ask. He opens with a statement about how much he appreciates the work that the mother does and thanks her for taking the time to schedule the meeting. He also talks about several strengths that Jackson possesses.

The team works together to update background information. The principal asks about any parental concerns. The mother shares that Jackson seems upset because the other students in his general education third-grade classroom are doing better than he, and she reports that he comes home crying 3 out of 5 days each week. His third-grade teacher, Mrs. Corell, voices her concern that he is falling further behind in the classroom. She is concerned that he is having difficulty processing auditory directions. He is only able to process a one-step direction and this is affecting how he is able to complete his assignments in class. The SLP then talks about how Jackson is doing in speech, and the special education teacher gives an update on how Jackson is doing with her.

Jackson's mom reports that she also sees problems with following directions at home. The team determines that they will develop a goal to work on two-step directions. The special education teacher will specifically work on this, and Jackson's time in special education will be increased by 30 minutes each day so that she can work one to one with him, specifically on strategies for following two-step directions. The SLP will work together with the special education teacher on specific strategies. For example, the SLP may be working on improving articulation and recommend the use of certain words in greetings, so the special education teacher can support this work by reinforcing the student when he is greeting someone using the correct terms. Or, the SLP might be working on pronunciation with a student, so she works together with the classroom teacher to come up with a list of words to include in the lesson, and the teacher can reinforce the student for utilizing the correct pronunciation. The classroom teacher agrees to only provide one-step directions to Jackson, although the special education teacher is working to teach him strategies for following two-step directions. They all agree to meet again in another 9 weeks to monitor Jackson's progress.

At the end of the meeting, the principal asks the special education teacher to review what she has typed into the computer for the updated IEP. She reviews it to see if she has captured what was said. All members agree with what she has recorded on the IEP, and the document is copied and disseminated before each participant leaves the meeting. Notice that the team members worked in a collaborative manner throughout this process. They communicated well and kept the needs of the student as their central focus.

SOLUTIONS TO COMMON MISTAKES

With the involvement of so many integral team members, mistakes or oversights can occur without careful attention to the intricacies of the IEP process. Here are the most common mistakes made regarding the IEP and their accompanying solutions.

Mistake: Transition discussions should occur as early as possible, and IDEA 2004 requires the involvement of outside agencies when the student reaches secondary school age. When considering the transition needs of a student at the appropriate age and grade level, school district personnel fail to invite the outside agencies who are responsible for providing services when the student exits the school system because they believe these agencies will not come.

Solution: The school district has the obligation to invite outside agencies, even if the individuals fail to attend. According to IDEA 2004, if a participating agency other than the local school district fails to provide the transition services described in the student's IEP, then the school district shall reconvene the IEP team to identify alternative strategies to meet the transition objectives set out by the IEP (20 U.S.C. 1414).

Mistake: Failure to include the student's general education teacher in the development of the BIP

Solution: IDEA 2004 includes a section about requirements with respect to the general education teacher. This section states that a student's general education teacher shall participate in the development of the IEP, including the determination of appropriate PBIS.

Mistake: A phenomena I call the revolving door IEP, particularly at the secondary level in which multiple teachers are involved: One teacher comes in, gives a report, and leaves; then another teacher comes in, gives a report, and leaves; and so forth. There is not one teacher who stays for the entire meeting, except for the special education teacher.

Solution: It is critical that at least one other teacher besides the special educator remains for the entire duration of the IEP meeting. If multiple teachers are unable to attend, then they can provide a written report that can be given by the one classroom teacher representative. A general education or content area teacher is an integral participant in the IEP process.

Mistake: Failure to record what was actually stated at the IEP meeting. I have had several experiences with this. The IEP team met and specifically determined that the student was not in need of a one-to-one paraprofessional. The teacher did not agree with the decision, and she went ahead and wrote in a one-to-one paraprofessional in the document because she was the one writing the IEP.

Solution: Develop ways for one or more people to proofread the IEP to make sure it reflects what was actually said. Provide training to the person recording the IEP about the importance of recording exactly what has been said. More schools are now using technology to project the working IEP onto a screen or developing other methods for sharing the document during the meeting. This gives everyone the opportunity to review the document as it is being typed.

Mistake: Developing an IEP that does not meet the stranger test. That is, a stranger from another school should be able to pick up the IEP and know what to do. I was attending an IEP meeting one day, and we were having an excellent discussion of the accommodations that the student needed. All agreed to the accommodations, but the individual recording the IEP document was not writing anything down. At a recess of the meeting, I asked the teacher why she was not recording any of the accommodations. She replied, "We make all these accommodations for all of the students in this school." Although that might have been true in this particular school, it may not be true if the student were to move. If a stranger in a new school district were to pick up the IEP, then he or she would not know that the student received any accommodations.

Solution: Carefully craft the IEP so that it is specific to the individual needs of that child. Ensure that all information concerning present levels of academic achievement and functional performance, as well as goals and objectives, are written in MOO terms. Carefully read over the IEP before disseminating it to make sure that someone who does not know the child could read it and have a clear understanding of the child's needs. Also, avoid the overuse of checklists. I have seen IEPs that were almost all checklists, and I read them and did not have a clue about the needs of the individual child. Some people will utilize an accommodations checklist and just check everything in case the student may need it. This is not very useful because someone may review it and think that the student needs all of the accommodations. Be cautious of checklists, especially if every student in a group has the same items checked, because that shows a lack of individualization.

Mistake: Showing up late for a student's IEP meeting

Solution: Work hard to be on time for a student's IEP meeting, and try to schedule it for a time when all or most participants can attend. Being late sends a bad message to the parents and others on the team—"I do not care enough about this student to be on time," or "I have more important things to do than be on time for this student's IEP meeting." This gets the IEP meeting off to a bad start and can create an adversarial situation with the parents.

Mistake: Scheduling too many IEP meetings in one day

Solution: Limit the number of IEP meetings that are scheduled in one day, and be careful to allow enough time between IEP meetings. Not only is there a possibility that meetings run over and subsequent meetings could be delayed, but the IEP team members also are exhausted and not likely to be at their best after several meetings throughout the day.

CHAPTER SUMMARY

The IEP is a living document meant to serve the student and provide for his or her future, created by a team of educational professionals with invaluable input on how to support the child in a variety of important areas. It is a plan for how to help the child succeed and thrive both in school and in life after the classroom. This chapter gave a practical overview of each stage of the IEP process, from conducting the IEP meeting and collaborating with parents to drafting and implementing the document. You have learned about the laws and regulations related to the IEP, including important time lines, required content, necessary input from the classroom teacher, and guidelines for revision.

So far this book has given you an understanding of your core responsibilities in educating students with disabilities and a foundation in the central laws governing special education. You now know the principles of the basic laws (IDEA 2004 and Section 504), the role of each educational team member, and the process of creating an educational program for each student. Now, it is time to learn more about your legal role in the classroom each day. The next chapter discusses the educator's responsibility to protect and supervise the children under his or her care.

Chapter 4 Extras and Activities

How to Advise? Tackling the Tough Questions in Special Education Law

Q: My child is in a special education class for three periods a day and receives speech-language and social work services. I am not happy about the social work services and want to revoke these services, but I am afraid I will lose the special education class and the speech-language services. What should I do?

A: As a parent, you may revoke the social work services for your child, and the school will not be able to implement those services. A more proactive plan, however, would be to meet with the case manager or building principal and ask for a new IEP meeting to discuss social work services. Then, follow your personal meeting up with a request in writing for the IEP meeting. You can outline your concerns at the IEP meeting. As an alternative, you may also want to meet with the social worker first and outline your concerns before you request a new IEP. You have the option of revoking the social work placement, but it is advisable to work collaboratively with school personnel to resolve your differences to ensure that your child gets the services he or she needs.

Apply Your Knowledge

1. Collect an IEP that has been written for a student (be sure to block out all identifying information so that there is not any way to identify the student). Critique the IEP by looking for the following:

   - Were the required participants present at the IEP team meeting?
   - Does the IEP address the strengths of the student?
   - Does the IEP provide enough information about the present levels of academic achievement and functional performance?
   - Does the IEP provide meaningful goals and objectives for the student that are written in MOO terms?
   - Are there options within the continuum of alternative placements discussed at the IEP?
   - What are the special considerations that were discussed in the IEP?

2. Critique whether these present levels of academic achievement and functional performance meet the MOO criteria, explain why or why not, and rewrite them for more specificity.

   - Jamar is misbehaving.
   - Dakota is truant.
   - Maria is a poor reader.
   - Mary Beth has difficulty in math at her grade level.

Interact

- Utilize a web site such as www.wrightslaw.com and find a case that deals with the IEP. Get into a group of peers/colleagues, and have group members discuss the case and whether they agree with the decision.
- Get into a small group and develop a sample agenda for an IEP meeting.

Read and Reflect

Observe an IEP meeting, or think about an IEP meeting that you have attended. What were some of the barriers to communication during the process, and what were the effective communication strategies that were utilized?

Online Activities

- *WebQuest:* Find three web sites that focus on writing appropriate IEPs, and summarize three key points from each of the web sites.

- Find a court case that deals with the development of an IEP, summarize the case, and state why you agree or disagree with the decision of the case.

Two Truths and a Lie*

Read all of these statements. Two are true, and one is a lie. Determine which one is a lie.

1. You should have three forms of written documentation to show that you have invited the parent to the IEP meeting.

2. If the parent revokes placement outlined in the IEP, then the school district cannot implement the placement.

3. If the general education teacher refuses to serve the student within the general education class, then the IEP team cannot place the student in the class.

*Answers for activities noted with an asterisk are provided in the Answer Key for Extras and Activities appendix.

5

Supervision and Protection of Students

In their role **in loco parentis** (Latin for "in the place of a parent"), school personnel have the obligation to act like the parent when protecting students from possible harm. School personnel must also assume responsibilities that parents do not have. School staff are charged with protecting children from abuse from other students and adults. They must also ensure that the constitutional rights of students are met (DeMitchell, 2012).

School personnel have a serious responsibility to monitor their students at all times. Documentation reveals that bullying persists in schools (U.S. Department of Education, 2014), and some children's misbehavior occurs when they believe that no one is watching (Johns & Carr, 2009). It may be in the restroom, in the hall, or in the cafeteria. It may be on the bus where there are high seats, and even though there are video cameras, those cameras cannot always catch what is going on in those seats. It may be when the students are at recess or are coming in from the bus or leaving school to catch the bus. Today's schools must be cognizant that they cannot leave students unsupervised. When something happens to a student and an adult does not see it, there are problems verifying what actually took place, and recounting the event can be inaccurate or up for dispute. A student can get seriously hurt, and there are no adult witnesses.

There are times when we think we are watching the students, but we are not. Picture the playground supervisors who are busy talking to each other when they are supposed to be watching the students. A student gets hit, and the supervisors do not see what happened. Picture the teacher who is escorting his or her students from the classroom to the cafeteria. The teacher decides to walk ahead of the students and cannot see what is happening behind him or her. Or, the teacher walks behind the class, and a few of the students run ahead. The teacher does not see what happens when a disturbance occurs.

Large groups of students congregated in one area can present problems. Pushing and shoving can occur in hallways when there are not enough adults supervising those areas. Students in the cafeteria may be engaging in inappropriate behavior under the table. They may be touching other students unbeknownst to the teachers. Schools are wise to identify areas in which behavior problems are occurring and then develop a plan to increase the supervision in those areas and at those times.

School personnel are also charged with making sure students are properly transported home. A student may get on the wrong bus, or a student may decide to go home with another student and the parent has not been told. All school staff need to know the transportation arrangements that are set for students and follow those plans.

BASIC PRINCIPLES OF THE LAWS AND REGULATIONS REGARDING STUDENT SUPERVISION

A review of cases related to discipline, abuse of students, and lack of supervision of students shows an increasing discussion about a provision in law known as Section 1983. (U.S.C., Title 42, Chapter 21, Section 1983)

> Every person who, under color of any statute, ordinance, regulation, custom, or usage, of any State or Territory or the District of Columbia, subjects, or causes to be subjected, any citizen of the United States or other person within the jurisdiction thereof to the deprivation of any rights, privileges, or immunities secured by the Constitution and laws, shall be liable to the party injured in an action at law, suit in equity, or other proper proceeding for redress, except that in any action brought against a judicial officer for an act or omission taken in such officer's judicial capacity, injunctive relief shall not be granted unless a declaratory decree was violated or declaratory relief was unavailable. (U.S.C., Title 42, Chapter 21, Section 1983)

Individuals who are employees of the school district may be personally sued if they violate the constitutional rights of children.

The family of a student with an IEP who has been harmed must exhaust the due process provisions of IDEA 2004. There are times, however, when claims of harm are not related to the provision of a FAPE. If injuries to a student are not educational in nature, then they cannot be remedied through the due process provisions of IDEA 2004.

For example, in a ruling by the Sixth Circuit Court (*F.H., by his next friend Sandra Fay Hall; Sandra Fay Hall v. Memphis City Schools; Vincent Hunter; Walter Banks; Malica Johnson; Patricia A. Toarmina; Pat Beane*, 2014), a student was diagnosed with cerebral palsy, asthma, auditory and visual limitations, and significant learning disorders. This child needed a wheelchair or walker for many years and had limited use of his hands. This made it difficult for him to be mobile and use the restroom without assistance. The parent had informed the staff of her son's needs. He attended four different schools over a period of years and had 11 different aides assigned to him. Among their responsibilities was to assist him in using the restroom. The student graduated in 2013. The family made several allegations of physical, sexual, and verbal abuse by the aides, including being left unattended and unsupervised in the restroom, which resulted in a seizure in one instance; being subjected to verbal and physical abuse from different aides and school personnel; being ridiculed about his disability; not receiving help to clean himself; and being sexually abused by an aide while in the bathroom.

The parent had proceeded through the IDEA 2004 due process system and reached a settlement agreement. The family later alleged that the district violated Section 1983 under the 14th Amendment of the Constitution, the Rehabilitation Act of 1973, and the ADA. The student had graduated from high school and sought compensation for injuries suffered at the hands of abusive aides. The Sixth Circuit Court pointed to noneducational injuries that have no available remedy under IDEA 2004, and, therefore, the parent could proceed and seek compensation.

The court ruled in *Payne ex rel. D.P. v. Peninsula Sch. Dist.* (2013) that a district can be liable under Section 1983 if the parent can show that an individual with policy-making authority ratified the staff's inappropriate conduct or if the school district had a practice of allowing such conduct to occur (Slater, 2014).

It was determined in *Kok ex rel. Estate of Kok v. Tacoma Sch. Dist.* (2013) that a school district cannot turn their back and ignore a student's history of violence or misconduct, but it was also determined that school personnel cannot be held liable for failing to predict behavior that is uncharacteristic of a student.

This chapter's How Would You Rule? exercise presents a devastating, true-life scenario in which a child died while in the school's care. How do you think the courts should have responded?

How Would You Rule?

A student suffocated on a school bus. The student had a neuromuscular condition and had trouble holding her head upright. It was necessary for her to be properly positioned on the bus. The need for proper positioning was outlined in her IEP. The parent and some school employees reported several times that some staff members were failing to appropriately position her to prevent any airway obstruction. The parent also had requested that the transportation staff be provided with more training. Was the district responsible for the child's suffocation?

Your ruling:

_____
_____
_____
_____
_____

The court's ruling:

The parent in *Herrera ex rel. Estate of I.H. v. Hillsborough County Sch. Board* (2013) alleged that district employees were deliberately indifferent to the student's disability-related needs. The district denied the claims and asked for a motion to dismiss, and the middle district of Florida denied the school district's motion. The court did not decide the truth of the claims but found that the district's reported failure to train staff on the importance of positioning could amount to deliberate indifference to the needs of the student with the disability.

It is clear that school personnel have a serious responsibility to protect and defend all students under their supervision and should be well trained and prepared

---

Just 3 X 5 It: A Mnemonic to Help You Remember

It is important that school personnel PROTECT children and their rights.

P—Parents: School personnel act in loco parentis when students are in school.

R—Responsibility: School personnel have a serious responsibility to supervise and protect the students within their care.

O—Observe: School personnel must observe their students at all times. There is greater risk of harm when students are not observed.

T—Treatment: Treatment of students should not place students in danger.

E—Evidence: Any time teachers have evidence that students are being abused or unsupervised, they have an obligation to report those instances.

C—Coverage: When taking students on field trips, ensure adequate coverage to provide the necessary supervision for the students entrusted to your care.

T—Training: Individuals should work to ensure that they have adequate training and that the staff they supervise have had training. It is important that school personnel PROTECT children and their rights.

---

to care for students with disabilities or special health care needs. This chapter's mnemonic is a reminder of this sacred duty.

CASE STUDY COMPARISON

Compare and contrast how students are supervised in the two scenarios described in this section. The first case study depicts the potentially tragic consequences of inadequate supervision, whereas the second example depicts some well-thought strategies for ensuring that students are safe.

A Case of Missteps and Mistakes

Jenny was a 9-year-old child who had a history of seizures and was enrolled in a class of students with multiple disabilities. One day, when Jenny came into school, her teacher noticed that she was not acting quite like herself. The teacher had the school nurse check on Jenny, and the school nurse called Jenny's mother to let her know that Jenny was not feeling well. Jenny's mother reported that Jenny had a seizure the night before and seemed lethargic this morning. The nurse assured Jenny's mother that they would keep an eye on Jenny to see if she continued to not feel well. The nurse reported the news to Jenny's teacher that Jenny had a seizure the evening before and was lethargic before she came to school. The nurse asked that the special education teacher monitor her to see if there was any change in Jenny's behavior.

Jenny was enrolled in a school that had a swimming pool, and the students were scheduled to go swimming in the afternoon for physical education. Her teacher decided that Jenny could go swimming because she did not seem to be feeling any worse by the time physical education was scheduled. The teacher, however, did not inform the physical education teacher of how Jenny had been acting that morning.

Three adults were usually in the pool with 10 students from two classes, but the physical education teacher was the only one in the pool with the students today. Jenny's special education teacher stood alongside the pool, as did another special education teacher and an assistant. They were talking with each other while the physical education teacher worked with the students. The physical education teacher did not notice that Jenny had gone underwater, nor did the three adults alongside the pool. It was too late by the time the physical education teacher did notice, and Jenny had stopped breathing. He got Jenny out of the pool and fortunately was able to resuscitate her. It was a close call, but Jenny survived.

What errors were made in this example? Consider the following lists of missteps and mistakes:

- There was not enough supervision in the pool considering all the students had multiple disabilities and the physical education teacher was the only one in the water. Jenny went underwater and stopped breathing while he was working with other students. More people should have been in the pool. Is the physical education teacher to blame? The teachers who were standing outside the pool were in loco parentis and had the responsibility to supervise and protect Jenny. They were talking and not attending to the students.

- Was it prudent for Jenny to go in the pool that day considering that she did not feel well that day and her mother reported that she had a seizure the night before? Should the special education teacher have consulted with the school nurse about whether Jenny should go in the pool? Yes, she should have. Did the physical education teacher have the **right to know** that Jenny had been lethargic that day and had a seizure the night before? Yes, the physical education teacher was being placed in the untenable position of watching 10 students with multiple disabilities in the pool. The physical education teacher had the right to know this information. If he would have known, then he could have voiced his belief that it was unsafe for Jenny to be in the pool or could have asked for additional assistance in the pool.

What could have been done to prevent this from happening to Jenny?

- The special education teacher should have consulted with the school nurse to determine whether it was safe for Jenny to go in the pool at all that day.

- If the nurse would have said that it was safe, then there should have been additional supervision of the students in the pool.

- The information about Jenny's seizure and lethargic behavior should have been shared with the physical education teacher because he may have asked for additional help in the pool or would have kept a much more watchful eye on Jenny.

The Exemplary Approach

Mrs. Krell, a fifth-grade teacher, has been teaching a unit on the life of Abraham Lincoln. She has worked closely with Mrs. Nolton, the SLP, and Mrs. Groves, the special education teacher, in planning the lessons to ensure that the students in special education have the necessary accommodations for the lessons. Both the special education teacher and the SLP have worked to build their students' vocabulary to understand the unit. They have developed mnemonics and other strategies to assist the students in remembering key points. A local theatre group is doing a play as a culmination of this activity, and it will be held during the school day but is 20 minutes away. Mrs. Krell has a concern—she is not sure she will be able to adequately supervise 27 fifth graders. She discusses the field trip with Mrs. Martinez, her building principal, who is a former teacher of students with emotional and behavior disorders. The principal approves the field trip. Mrs. Martinez says she will check her schedule to see if she can go. If she cannot go, then she will put a call out for those in the substitute teacher pool to see if any of them would be willing to volunteer that day. Mrs. Martinez also suggests Mrs. Krell talk to the SLP and special education teacher to see whether they can go on the trip. Both are excited to go and make sure to contact the parents of the other students they see during the time of the play to let them know that they will make up their work with the students during that week. Mrs. Martinez is able to clear her schedule and talks with Mrs. Krell about developing a plan for supervising all the students. Two of the substitutes in the building volunteer to go on the field trip, so six adults will be going on the trip with the students. The teachers and the principal will each be responsible for the supervision of five students. One of the volunteers will watch four students, and the other will watch three students.

Mrs. Krell prepares the students for the play and explains the rules for the field trip. The teacher and principal explain the rules again to the students when they get on the bus, and they let the students know the adult that will be supervising them. Students are expected to stay with their assigned staff member at all times. Students will go to the restroom with their group's staff member. One student at a time will go into the restroom after the adult has checked to make sure there is no one else in the restroom. If anyone needs to go to the restroom at another time, then the person assigned to the student will take the student and let the other staff know so they can watch the other students. The staff member will again check the restroom to make sure no one else is in there.

Students are reinforced for appropriate behavior, and if students fail to follow staff directions, then they will be given one warning. If they misbehave a second time, then the bus driver and principal will take the student to the bus, where the student will remain for a period of 15 minutes. The students that the principal was supervising will be watched by another individual. The student will then return to the play. If the same student misbehaves again, then the student will again be returned to the bus, where he or she will remain until the trip is over.

SOLUTIONS TO COMMON MISTAKES

The following mistakes should be avoided to ensure students' safety and care.

Mistake: Failure to provide adequate supervision in all educational settings

Solution: School personnel must be careful to ensure that they are supervising their students at all times. This is not easy at all. Students may run ahead when they are in line or may lag behind so that the teacher cannot see them, which is an invitation for problems such as bullying. Students with disabilities are bullied at a higher rate than students without disabilities (U.S. Department of Education, 2014; see Chapter 6). Students are more likely to be bullied when an adult is not watching. All school personnel are charged with the serious obligation of providing a safe and secure environment, and they have to be able to watch their students and monitor their behavior in order to provide that environment. I worked for many years with students who were sex offenders, and I had to watch them very carefully because they would try to engage in inappropriate behaviors under the tables in the cafeteria. They would watch for an opportunity when an adult was not looking to attempt to engage in inappropriate behavior. The following are some recommendations for monitoring students:

- Educators should meet with their administration when they are concerned that they are not able to provide enough supervision for their students in order to develop a plan for supervision.

- School personnel who notice an increase in bullying behaviors should identify the target areas of the school or the bus in which these behaviors are reported to be occurring and develop a plan for increased supervision in those areas.

- Schools may place video cameras in parts of classrooms or on the bus and think that it will solve all of the problems of supervision. This is important to do in some situations, but it will not answer all of the issues with supervision. Video cameras are positioned to pick up certain areas of the bus, but the students are smart enough to figure out how to engage in behaviors that will not be seen on the video. Even though video cameras are in place in school hallways, there may still be blind spots, and schools should identify those blind spots and ensure that they have supervision in those areas.

- The IEP team needs to develop a plan for increased supervision when the IEP is developed for a student who has a history of bullying or sexually deviant behavior. The team should carefully review the needs and past history of the student to see how, when, and where the student may be likely to have problems and create a plan for supervision at critical times.

- School personnel should be listening closely to what students are saying. Are they fearful of certain situations? Does one student's name keep coming up as the one who is engaging in bullying?

Mistake: Failure to assign supervisory responsibilities to specific individuals when field trips are taken or when there are large-group activities

Solution: A sufficient number of staff members should be assigned to accompany students on field trips. Individuals should be assigned the responsibility of supervising particular students on that trip. In another case I reviewed, a student was allowed to go to a public restroom unaccompanied. There was another student in the restroom at the same time. That student was also unaccompanied. The sad part of this story was that one student raped the other student, and no adult could figure out what happened because no one knew where either of these students was at the time. Adults need to be careful about restrooms. If students are fearful of going to a restroom in the school, then educators need to find out why. They may be bullied in the restroom. If educators are getting complaints about a student's behavior, then they should not allow other students in the restroom at the same time.

Mistake: Failure to identify physical blind spots within the building where it is hard to see what students are doing

Solution: As previously mentioned, even when schools provide video cameras, there are certain blind spots in buildings, on buses, on the playground, and in the cafeteria where students are not being observed. Some students will take advantage of this opportunity and engage in inappropriate behaviors. A major problem occurs when large numbers of students are passing in the hall at one time or too many students are in the cafeteria together. When that is the case, school personnel may need to investigate options, such as staggered passing times in the hall or decreased numbers in the cafeteria. Students may be bullied when they leave school. If this is happening outside of the school grounds, then educators must recognize this and take action to make this environment equally safe for the students.

Mistake: Failure to train individuals who are responsible for supervising students

Solution: Educators must be trained on the importance of supervision, how to supervise, what to do when witnessing inappropriate behavior, and to whom instances of inappropriate behavior should be reported. Training volunteers, playground supervisors, cafeteria workers, bus drivers, substitutes, and other individuals who may be responsible for the supervision of students is equally important. Communicate to these individuals that they are all responsible for supervision and cannot ignore inappropriate behavior. I have seen playground supervisors clustered in a group talking while the children were engaging in bullying behavior on the playground. Volunteers or others may sometimes be afraid to intervene to stop the behavior because they do not know what to do. School administration must stress the seriousness of their role and give them a plan for what should be done when they see inappropriate behavior.

CHAPTER SUMMARY

This chapter presented important strategies for ensuring student safety and well-being in every aspect of the school day. All school personnel are responsible for supervising children to keep them free from harm, in effect assuming a parental role during school hours. They have a legal responsibility to ensure that none of the students' rights are violated and closely monitor student behavior. The following chapter more deeply discusses the educator's role in addressing student behavior, with a particular emphasis on intervening to help students struggling with behavioral challenges as a result of a disability.

Chapter 5 Extras and Activities

How to Advise? Tackling the Tough Questions in Special Education Law

Q: My child has seizures, and I am concerned about the possibility of seizures when the teacher is not with him. I am worried about what will happen if he has a seizure with a substitute or has a seizure in the cafeteria or on the bus. I have talked with the principal, and he says that he is unable to tell other people because my child has the right to his privacy. Is this right?

A: If a staff member is working with a student with a disability and is responsible for that child's care during a specific period of time, then that individual needs to know the important information about the student that could affect the child in his or her care. In this example, it is possible that the student may experience a seizure in the cafeteria or on the bus. The staff need to be trained on what to do in such an event. They also must be taught specific laws related to **confidentiality** so that they are not sharing the information with individuals who do not need to know.

Interact

- The following is a variation of dominoes that is fun to play with a group and provides the opportunity to move around the room and interact. Make matching sets of cards for the individuals who are participating in the activity.

  - Write "in loco" on one card and "parentis" on the other card.

  - Write "deliberate" one on card and "indifference" on the other card.

  - Write "compensatory" on one card and "damages" on the other card.

  - Write "right" on one card and "to know" on the other card.

- Each individual is given a card. Everyone mingles around the room and partners with the person who has the matching card. The partners discuss their term and come up with a creative way to teach it to others, such as a picture, poem, or skit. Depending on the size of the group, each pair can share what they have done with the others, or three to four pairs can be selected to present.

Apply Your Knowledge

Identify five areas in your school where there are blind spots that make it difficult to see the students. Brainstorm solutions for increasing supervision in these blind spots. If you are a preservice teacher, then observe in a school, identify five areas where there are blind spots, and provide suggestions on what the school might do to provide more supervision.

Online Activities

- *WebQuest:* Find a web site that deals with school safety. Investigate whether the site covers the topic of supervision of students, and, if so, what five helpful hints does it provide?

- Find a court case in which a teacher was personally sued because he or she violated a child's constitutional rights. Then, describe the case and whether you agree with the decision.

Two Truths and a Lie*

Read all of these statements. Two are true, and one is a lie. Determine which one is a lie.

1. A teacher who has exhibited intent to harm that could threaten a child's constitutional rights cannot be personally sued, but the school district itself can be sued.

2. Individuals who work within the school district and who work with the student and have a right to know should be informed of critical information about the student.

3. When a paraprofessional engages in harmful actions toward a child, such as blowing a whistle in a child's ear, the teacher has the responsibility to stop the behavior.

*Answers for activities noted with an asterisk are provided in the Answer Key for Extras and Activities appendix.

6

Implementing Appropriate Behavioral Interventions

It is very common for students with disabilities or those who have IEPs to exhibit some kind of challenging behavior. A common misconception is that BIPs are only developed for students who have been identified as having emotional disturbance; this is not the case. Many students who have autism, intellectual disabilities, learning disabilities, or any other disability also may have behavior that hinders learning. IDEA 2004 and its accompanying regulations require that the IEP team consider using PBIS and other strategies to address a child's behavior that impedes the child's learning or others' learning (34 C.F.R. 300.324).

The behaviors interfering with learning can have a number of different functions for the student and present themselves differently, depending on that student's disability and unique challenges. Students receiving services within the emotional disturbance category are referred for special education because their internalizing or externalizing behaviors interfere with learning. Students with autism and/or Asperger syndrome are characterized by difficulties with communication as well as impairments in social interaction (O'Connor & Stichter, 2011), whereas children with intellectual disabilities exhibit problems in adaptive behavior. Students with learning disabilities may have behavioral challenges related to their problems with processing information and directions (Lerner & Johns, 2015). Under IDEA 2004, any student whose behavior impedes learning should have a preventive, positive, and proactive BIP that is based on a **functional behavioral assessment (FBA).** Just as a student's academic program should be based on a thorough evaluation, the same is true of a BIP. Educators have to understand why the student is engaging in inappropriate behaviors in order to effectively intervene.

BIPs are based on positive strategies designed to make long-term changes in behavior. The FBA is best conducted by a team of individuals who are knowledgeable in curriculum, instruction, and behavior. Behaviors always serve a purpose, and the function of behavior might be gaining access, escaping/avoiding, or addressing sensory needs. Some children engage in behavior to escape from academic tasks that might be too difficult for them or that are presented in a manner that does not meet their needs. As a result, it is important that instruction and its relationship to behavior be explored. When academic tasks become difficult, some students will respond with disruptive behavior that gets them removed from the classroom or even suspended from school (Johns & Carr, 2012).

EFFECTIVE SCHOOL DISCIPLINE

School personnel too often think that suspension is the only way to deal with students with behavioral challenges. The zero tolerance policy was originally designed so that any infraction of the rules would lead to punishment, regardless of extenuating circumstances. Suspension is too often considered the answer, and students are removed from school for misbehavior. A mistaken notion is that suspension is a punishment and it changes behavior. Suspension is a reward, however, for many students, many of whom may be struggling in school as a result of learning disabilities, because they do not want to attend school in the first place. In fact, suspension can result in increased inappropriate behavior because students who do not want to be in school set themselves up to be suspended as a means of escaping. Research shows that one third of students with learning disabilities are suspended or expelled from school one or more times (Cortiella, 2011).

Because suspension is a frequent means of discipline for students, there are many debates about how many days a student can be suspended, what constitutes a day of suspension, whether the behavior is related to the disability, and what happens when the student has exceeded 10 days of suspension. These discussions could be significantly curtailed if suspension was not utilized as an intervention. Implementing MTSS, in which behavioral expectations are made clear for all students and universal instruction or supports (Tier 1) are delivered, is one way schools are addressing the topic of suspension as an intervention. Schoolwide positive behavior interventions and supports (SWPBIS) focus on providing reinforcement for appropriate behavior as opposed to focusing on punitive measures that only provide negative consequences for inappropriate behavior. For example, if schools are facing increased behavior problems in the hallway, then they can teach the students expectations for hallway behavior, and they can establish increased adult supervision in the hall. Those supervisors use positive reinforcement to recognize students for following the hallway expectations. Students who continue to struggle with regulating their behavior are targeted for a small-group, or Tier 2, intervention. Finally, individualized interventions, such as an FBA or a BIP, are implemented for those who continue to exhibit challenging behavior; these are referred to as Tier 3 interventions. A reduction in challenging behaviors occurs when school personnel address them in a positive way by meeting the individual needs of students and recognizing students for appropriate behavior. PBIS or MTSS have been shown to reduce the need for suspension.

Whether there should be a federal law about the use of seclusion and restraint is another area of school discipline up for discussion. Some states have laws that govern when and under what conditions either time-out or physical restraint can be used. Seclusion should only be utilized under specific conditions and directed or supervised only by qualified personnel. In the absence of federal laws and regulations, it is critical that educators proceed with caution in the use of such procedures. It is outside the purview of this book to provide details on appropriate use of restrictive procedures. Educators should know what procedures are being used within their state and their school district. The IEP team must look at the effectiveness of such a restrictive intervention when it is being utilized too often. It is the obligation of the IEP team to ensure that the intervention is being done with fidelity (Johns, 2014).

It is critical that educators understand their role in discipline as threefold: Fairness in discipline, education of students, and protection of students. It is critical that educators are being fair to students when they are implementing disciplinary procedures such as consequences and suspension. The U.S. Department of Justice and the U.S. Department of Education (2014) issued a letter to school personnel to provide guidance on fairness in discipline. They stressed that schools must administer school discipline without discriminating on the basis of race, color, or national origin. That letter pointed out that African American students are disciplined more harshly and more frequently, and students with significant behavioral issues are more likely to be suspended or expelled (Wehby & Kern, 2014).

The importance of educating students is the second factor to consider. We must teach students how to behave and the consequences for misbehavior. Teachers use Tier 1 of PBIS or MTSS to establish clear rules and guidelines for appropriate behavior starting on the first day of school. The rules are clearly stated and posted around the school and classrooms. Teachers may also use some proactive approaches to teaching social skills. Keeping students in class so they can learn these social skills, as well as academic skills, is critical.

Protection of students is the third factor of school discipline. We must keep students safe in schools (see Chapter 5). Although educators cannot protect students from all negative situations, they can be alert to problem situations in which students do not feel safe, especially if they may be victims of bullying (see Box for

---

 Ways School Personnel Can Prevent Bullying

Cases involving the bullying of students are frequently seen in the press. Students with disabilities are bullied or harassed more than their typically developing peers (U.S. Department of Education, 2014). How do school personnel stop this rising trend? This can be done in several ways:

- Instruct students in appropriate social skills that include how to treat peers with respect. Send the message that bullying is never acceptable.

- Reinforce students who are engaging in positive, appropriate behavior.

- Require that students report every instance of bullying or harassment that they see to any teacher, administrator, or adult.

- Educators should not ignore any reports of bullying. When bullying is ignored by adults, the message to students is that it is acceptable to bully.

- Supervision of students is critical for preventing students with disabilities from becoming victims of bullying.

- Follow the Golden Rule: Treat others as you want them to treat you and those around you. We model appropriate behavior when we treat others with respect.

- If your school does not already have a system to track or investigate reports of bullying, then consider starting one. It can provide students with a feeling of safety or protection without fear of retaliation.

core bullying prevention strategies that can be implemented in school). The foundation for a safe school is in place when standard behavioral practices and positive reinforcement are implemented.

Challenging behaviors can be curtailed by systematically planning a positive and preventive approach, providing the supports for school personnel that are required by IDEA 2004, and having a continuum of alternative placements to meet the needs of diverse students. Supports for school personnel may mean that the teacher needs additional training in the area of behavior management or needs additional coaching. The teacher may also need additional assistance within the classroom. The continuum of alternative placements involves school districts providing an array of placement options, not just a separate class or a regular class without supports (see Chapter 3). A student will need the necessary supports to meet his or her needs, regardless of the setting in which he or she is educated.

BASIC PRINCIPLES OF THE LAWS AND REGULATIONS REGARDING DISCIPLINE AND BEHAVIOR

By law, the IEP team must consider PBIS and other strategies to address behavior in the case of a child whose behavior impedes learning (34 C.F.R. 300.524). The general education teacher, as a member of the IEP team, must, to the extent appropriate, participate in determining appropriate PBIS and other strategies for the child as well as supplementary aids and services, program modifications, and support for school personnel (34 C.F.R. 300.324). This is important to remember as the needs of students with challenging behaviors are discussed because it is critical that the classroom teacher is an integral part of the discussion about behavioral interventions, especially if the student is spending time within that classroom. Supports for school personnel could include training for the classroom teacher, special education teacher, or classroom assistant. A discussion of the supports that are necessary in meeting the goals and objectives for a student is needed when the teacher is concerned about working with a student with challenging behaviors.

What does IDEA 2004 say about suspension? School personnel "may remove a child with a disability who violates a code of student conduct from his or her current placement to an appropriate **interim alternative educational setting,** another setting, or suspension for not more than 10 consecutive school days (to the extent that those alternatives are applied to children without disabilities)" (34 C.F.R. 300.530). In other words, there cannot be a stricter consequence for students with disabilities than for those without disabilities. I can remember a district superintendent calling me about a student with a disability who was caught with drugs, and the superintendent wanted to place the student in an interim alternative educational setting for 45 school days. I asked the superintendent what the consequence was for a student without disabilities if he or she were in possession of drugs at school. He replied that it would be a 5-day suspension. I had to tell him that he could not impose a stricter consequence for a student with a disability than what was in place for students without disabilities. School districts are only required to provide services during periods of removal for 10 days or less if it provides services to a child without disabilities who is removed in a similar way.

After a child with a disability has been removed from his or her current placement for 10 school days in the same school year, the school must provide services during any subsequent days of removal. When discipline involving suspension exceeds 10 school days, services still must be provided, even if the behavior is not determined to be a manifestation of the disability.

This becomes a **change of placement because of disciplinary removals**. A change of placement occurs if the removal of a student with a disability is "for more than ten consecutive school days" (34 C.F.R. 300.536) or "the child has been subjected to a series of removals that constitute a pattern" (34 C.F.R. 300.536).

Those services, when there is a **change of placement because of disciplinary removals**, must enable the child to continue to participate in the general education curriculum and progress toward meeting the IEP goals, but in another setting. The student must also receive an FBA and behavioral intervention services and modifications that address the behavior so that it does not reoccur. The services may be provided in an interim alternative educational setting (34 C.F.R. 300.530).

How is a **manifestation determination** done? The local district, parent, and relevant members of the IEP team must convene to review all relevant information in the child's file, the behavior incident, observations of the student's behavior, and any other relevant details provided by the parent to determine if 1) the conduct was caused by or had a direct and substantial relationship to the child's disability and 2) if the conduct in question was the direct result of the district's failure to implement the IEP. If the behavior was a manifestation of the child's disability, then the IEP team must conduct an FBA, unless one has already been completed before the behavior occurred, and implement a BIP for the child. If a BIP has already been developed, then it has to be reviewed and modified as necessary. The child is then returned to his or her original placement unless the parent and district agree to a change in placement (34 C.F.R. 300.530).

Different rules apply, however, if a student brings a weapon to school, knowingly transports drugs, or has inflicted serious bodily injury on him- or herself or others. In this situation, school personnel may remove a student to an interim alternative educational setting for not more than 45 school days, regardless of whether the behavior was related to the disability. The IEP team determines the interim alternative educational setting. Notice is given to the parent on the date the decision is made to move the student to the interim alternative educational setting. Notice must also include the procedural safeguards (34 C.F.R. 300.530). Procedural safeguards are a set of rights for parents based on IDEA 2004, including the right to due process, the right to an evaluation of their child, the right to review and have access to student records, the right to be involved in the IEP, the right to receive regularly scheduled progress reports, and the opportunity to present and resolve complaints (see Chapter 2). The student moves to the interim alternative educational setting, but the parent may appeal the decision through an expedited hearing, and the hearing officer makes the final decision. In the meantime, the student remains in the interim alternative educational setting (34 C.F.R. 300.532).

School districts do have the right to consider the individual needs of students by making a **case-by-case determination**. IEP teams may consider any unique circumstances on a case-by-case basis when determining whether a change in placement is appropriate for a child with a disability who violates a code of student conduct, as long as the determination made is within the specific discipline regulations of IDEA 2004. As an example, the team might decide that the student will only move to an interim alternative educational setting for 30 days or the team might determine that an interim alternative educational setting is not appropriate for the student.

Does a student who has not been identified as having a disability have any rights afforded to students with disabilities? If there was **basis of knowledge**, then the student does have rights. If a child has not been identified as a student with a disability and engages in behavior that is a violation of the code of conduct, then that student can assert any of the protections of the Individuals with Disabilities Education Improvement Act (IDEA) of 2004 (PL 108-446) if school personnel had the **basis of knowledge** before the behavior that precipitated the disciplinary action, as exhibited by the following:

"The parent of the child expressed concern in writing to supervisory or administrative personnel of the appropriate educational agency or a teacher that the child is in need of special education and related services" (34 C.F.R. 300.534).

"The parent of the child requested an evaluation of the child" (34 C.F.R. 300.534).

"The teacher of the child, or other personnel, had expressed specific concerns about a pattern of behavior demonstrated by the child directly to the director of special education or other supervisory personnel" (34 C.F.R. 300.534).

There are exceptions, including if the parent refused an evaluation or refused services or if the child was evaluated and determined not to be a student with a disability.

Police intervention is allowed under IDEA 2004. Nothing in the law prohibits the school district from reporting a crime committed by a child with a disability to the police, and nothing prohibits state law enforcement and judicial authorities from exercising their responsibilities when a crime is committed by a student with a disability. School districts should have policies and procedures on the appropriate use of police intervention and should meet with police in advance and seek their assistance in developing policies and procedures. Johns (2014) outlined procedures about calling the police in cases in which crimes have been committed.

- Establish a working relationship with police departments.

- Avoid having multiple people call the police when a crime has been committed.

- Exercise extreme caution when using students as witnesses.

- Know where the crime was committed.

This chapter's mnemonic helps you remember the most important guidelines for improving and addressing student behavior in your school.

This chapter's "How Would You Rule?" exercise invites you to think about how school systems should respond to student behavior problems and what supports should be provided.

How Would You Rule?

Staff members raised concerns that a 10th-grade student had a pattern of challenging behaviors. The student had a Section 504 accommodation plan because he had been hospitalized for attempted suicide, had failing grades, and could not stay in class. The school district administration argued that the district did not have knowledge that the student had a disability, even though the assistant principal

---

Just 3 X 5 It: A Mnemonic to Help You Remember

Help keep students on their best BEHAVIOR by doing the following.

B—Build positive relationships with students.

E—Expectations must be set.

H—How to behave: Students must know how to behave in each setting.

A—Assess the function of the behavior.

V—Value and respect each individual student.

I—Intervene when challenging behaviors first occur.

O—Observe behavior to better understand it.

R—Reinforce appropriate behavior.

---

attended the accommodation plan meeting in which the teachers discussed the student's panic attacks and inability to complete work. The student was suspended for violating school rules, and the district did not conduct a manifestation determination. The administration said there had not been a request for an evaluation, and, therefore, the student was not entitled to a manifestation determination. The parent argued that the district should have completed a case study evaluation and that the young man was a child with a disability under IDEA 2004. Do you think that the school system should have completed a manifestation determination?

Your ruling:

_____

_____

_____

_____

_____

The court's ruling:

The court ruled in *Anaheim Union High Sch. Dist. v. J.E.* (2013) that the assistant principal did attend the Section 504 meeting and heard the concerns of the teachers, even though they did not specifically request a case study evaluation. This knowledge and information required the school to conduct a manifestation determination related to the suspension. Staff at the school suspected the student had a disability because he had a 504 plan. Even though the young man was not yet found eligible for IDEA 2004 services, he was still eligible for services and the procedural safeguards of IDEA 2004 because the teachers voiced concerns that showed that the behavior had an adverse impact on his education.

This case reminds educators that behavioral challenges must be taken seriously, regardless of whether a student has a label or diagnosis of a disability. If a student is suspected of having a disability, then the school district has an obligation to conduct an evaluation.

CASE STUDY COMPARISON

School personnel in the first case study fail to properly address behavioral challenges of students and show a misunderstanding of the law, leading to legal consequences for the school. Compare this example with the exemplary approach of utilizing a system of SWPBIS.

A Case of Missteps and Mistakes

Mrs. Abion teaches an instructional class for students with emotional and behavior disorders at Perry High School, a school of about 1500 students. She works closely with the social worker and school psychologist to create a positive school environment for her students. She also integrates most of her students to the maximum extent appropriate in general education classes according to the provisions of the students' IEPs. She utilizes effective PBIS that have been delineated in each of her students' IEPs. These interventions are based on an FBA.

Dustin, a ninth-grade student, is doing well in her classroom when he is at school. She is concerned, however, because the dean and assistant principal keep suspending him based on behavior that occurs between the time he gets off the school bus and comes into the building. It is now November, and Dustin has missed 15 days of school because of this behavior.

The first time the assistant principal suspended Dustin, Mrs. Abion talked with the principal and explained that she would like a new IEP meeting to discuss this behavior and come up with a BIP for this particular behavior. She was eager to establish a positive recognition system for Dustin when he was behaving well. Mrs. Abion has other students whom she supervises during the time when Dustin is coming into the building; otherwise, she would be happy to supervise him. Both the school psychologist and social worker offer to help during the problematic time, but the assistant principal says he can handle the situation. After 4 more days of suspension, Mrs. Abion returns to the assistant principal offering to help, as do the social worker and school psychologist. The assistant principal becomes agitated and says he handles discipline at this time and that he does not need their assistance. Mrs. Abion documents her conversation in writing, as does the social worker and the school psychologist.

The assistant principal is absent one day, and the dean is on supervision during this time. The assistant principal in the school is responsible for attendance and academic initiatives. The dean in the school is responsible for maintaining discipline and order. Dustin is swearing when he comes in the building. The dean tells him he will not tolerate this, and the dean suspends Dustin for 5 days. At this point, Mrs. Abion goes to the building principal and requests a new IEP team meeting for Dustin. She documents this in writing. She is feeling very frustrated. The principal says he will see what he can do, but he is busy and explains that Dustin needs to learn to follow the rules. When Dustin returns to school after the 5-day suspension, he walks in swearing, and the assistant principal suspends Dustin another 5 days. He has now received 15 days of suspension. The parents file a due process hearing on behalf of their son based on the number of suspension days. The principal comes to Mrs. Abion upset and says that the IEP team will need to reconvene to conduct a manifestation determination. The principal claims that the situation is ridiculous and his administrative team has the right to suspend a student as many days as they want.

Both parents and their attorney attend the IEP manifestation determination. The school attorney asks Mrs. Abion why she has not developed a BIP to keep these events from occurring. Mrs. Abion is very factual and explains the actions she has taken, providing the written evidence of what she has tried to do. The parent attorney also asks the same questions of the school social worker and the school psychologist. They share their written documentation as well. When asked if they believe that Dustin's behavior is a manifestation of his disability, the teacher, social worker, and school psychologist all relay that Dustin has ADHD and engages in oppositionally defiant behaviors, so the swearing is related to his disability.

The parents' attorney asks the principal, assistant principal, and dean why they have continued to suspend Dustin. They explain that they have the right to conduct the disciplinary interventions that they choose because they are administrators. The school board's attorney talks with the school staff and administrators privately and lets them know that they will need to settle this case because they have exceeded the 10 days of suspension and have failed to create an effective BIP for behavior directly related to Dustin's disability.

What errors were made in this example? Consider the following lists of missteps and mistakes:

- The administrators failed to monitor the number of days of suspension that Dustin received.

- The administrators believed that they were in charge of discipline and did not recognize that a special education student's BIP is part of the student's IEP.

- The administrators did not understand the importance of PBIS.

- The principal failed to reconvene the IEP team when Mrs. Abion, the psychologist, and the school social worker made the request. Three staff members requested a new IEP meeting, and the principal still did not schedule one.

What could be done to prevent this from reoccurring?

- The principal, assistant principal, and dean need to attend trainings to understand the discipline provisions of IDEA 2004. They also need training in appropriate behavior management techniques and alternatives to suspension.

- The school system needs a tracking system for suspensions. When multiple individuals are suspending students from school, it is critical to monitor these occurrences so that the school can take needed action before the student approaches 10 days of suspension.

- The special education teacher, social worker, and school psychologist took the right steps by talking with the administrators and documenting the conversations in writing. They should continue openly communicating with administrators and keeping a record of this communication.

The Exemplary Approach

Mrs. Imperioli is the principal of Gardens High School, which has approximately 1500 students. Gardens had a high suspension rate and many challenging behaviors 6 years ago. About 60% of the students had office referrals during the year. When Mrs. Imperioli took over as high school principal, she knew she had to make changes. She did not believe in suspending students. She knew that many of the students wanted to get kicked out. She began laying the foundation for implementing SWPBIS in her first year as principal. She formed a committee of key staff members and provided them with a great deal of training on SWPBIS. She also did extensive training with all of the staff on alternatives to suspension.

Mrs. Imperioli and a team of individuals closely investigated the office referrals that were occurring and where they originated. She saw that there were two second-year teachers who were sending students to the office more than all the others combined. Rather than blaming these teachers, she worked closely with them to determine their needs and what was precipitating the office referrals. She provided extensive behavior management training and coaching to these two teachers. The school psychologist and school social worker spent time in the teachers' classrooms coaching and supporting them. Those teachers' office referrals had been significantly reduced within 4 months.

Once the committee had received training on SWPBIS, there was extensive training of all staff in order to implement the system. A great deal of excitement emanated from the staff because they all knew how much support that the two struggling teachers had received. They knew that Mrs. Imperioli would work together with them to implement the system. Parents were also informed of the new changes occurring in the school. Mrs. Imperioli stressed that she wanted to keep their kids in school and wanted to work with them to do so. She communicated positively with families and stressed that teachers should inform parents when the students were doing well. Finally, outside agencies who worked closely with the school were informed of what was happening in the building. Some businesses in town contributed to the positive incentives that were associated with SWPBIS.

Although the system was working well with the majority of students, Mrs. Imperioli worked closely with her special education staff on meeting the needs of the children who would be considered the Tier 3 students, those students who have multiple needs and require a wide array of placement options and support services. There were resource services and self-contained programming within the special education program for those students who needed those parts of the continuum. The staff worked hard to achieve interagency collaboration to meet the mental health needs of the students and provide the comprehensive services the students needed. Evidence-based interventions were provided to all students within the school's MTSS. If those interventions were not sufficient to meet the needs of the student, then the student would receive more targeted supports in Tier 2. If those supports were inadequate, then the student was referred for special education or entitled to individualized supports (Tier 3).

There were no out-of-school suspensions, and an in-school suspension system, along with a complete system of earned privileges and logical consequences for inappropriate behavior, had been established within the second year of implementing SWPBIS.

SOLUTIONS TO COMMON MISTAKES

Read about the most common mistakes in approaching students' behavioral challenges, with accompanying solutions to broaden your understanding of how to implement discipline and appropriate support.

Mistake: Failure to understand the function of a student's behavior

Solution: We may take the easy way out and assume the student's behavior is for a given reason, only to find out we were wrong. For instance, we may assume the student is doing something to get attention when that student is really engaging in an inappropriate behavior because he or she is overwhelmed by a task that he or she perceives to be too difficult for him or her.

Mistake: When we are working with a student, it is easy for us to get too close to the situation and not see what is really going on

Solution: FBA is more effective when a team approach is utilized because what one person misses, another person might catch. An effective FBA thoroughly looks at the function of the behavior, medical implications of the behavior, whether the child has learned the appropriate behaviors for specific situations, and analyzes the ABCs of the behavior—the antecedents (what happens before the behavior), the behavior (described in operational terms), and the consequences (what happens after the behavior).

Mistake: A one-size-fits-all behavior management approach. I still see BIPs that are checklists of strategies, and all of the students in the group have the same strategies marked for them. Just like one-size-fits-all clothes do not work for everyone, the same behavioral interventions do not work for all students.

Solution: Children have individualized needs, and behaviors are complex. An FBA must be conducted in order to plan an effective BIP. The academic, medical, and social needs of a student must be understood in order to plan an effective BIP. The child may be misbehaving because he or she does not know the appropriate behavior, and the behavior has to be taught. Research must be done on effective behavioral interventions that exist, and these interventions are then implemented based on the needs of the student. If the chosen intervention is not working, then the team should meet again to review whether the intervention was implemented with fidelity and determine the specific reasons why the intervention may not be working.

Mistake: Failure to understand our role in the behavior problems of students

Solution: We have to be able to thoroughly review our own behavior and determine whether we may be causing the student's challenging behaviors. Are members of the team getting into power struggles with students? Do we become easily agitated with the student and the student knows that? When there is a problem with a student, we need to start by looking at ourselves. It can be tough for us to admit that we might be part of the problem; however, it is important to analyze and rectify our own behavior if it is contributing to a student's challenges.

Mistake: Failure to understand that some challenging behaviors are specific to certain disabilities and that the student's developmental level affects their behavior. For instance, students with ASD may have some executive function challenges and cannot attend to directions, or a 10-year-old student with an intellectual disability may be included with his or her peers in fourth grade but is at the developmental level of a much younger student. For example, if a child has a learning disability that has resulted in delayed auditory processing time, then allowances must be made for the student to have more time to process directions. It would be too easy to assume the student is refusing to respond because he or she is not answering right away, when, in fact, it is the child's processing delay that is prohibiting him or her from immediately carrying out the directions.

Solution: The student's individual needs must be reviewed as part of the FBA. We have to ask ourselves the following questions:

- What is the student's social-emotional level?

- Does the student's receptive/expressive language levels affect the behavior?

- Can the student process the directions that are given?

- Does the student know how to behave in a certain situation?

- Is the student's behavior affected by the environment, including the setting, other students, or particular adults? I remember a student who was misbehaving because there was a mobile that was dangling above his desk, and the swaying movement was bothering him.

- Are there sensory reasons the student may be misbehaving? For example, there may be too much noise, too much light or not enough light, or a bothersome smell in the room.

- Is the student bringing emotional baggage from a previous situation? The student may have had trouble in math the previous year. Even though the new math teacher is an excellent one who makes math engaging and motivating, the student still associates math with a bad experience. Or, the student may have had a fight with mom before coming to school.

Mistake: Failure to have a continuum of placement options for students with behavioral challenges

Solution: Inclusion may have caused exclusion for some students. In some people's zeal to place all students with disabilities in general education classes, they fail to look at options for students. The general education environment may be appropriate for some students, but it may not be for some others. Some students with significant emotional or behavioral challenges need a more protected environment and do better in a smaller group in which they can get specialized support. Schools need to ensure that they have a range of placement options for their students. There are students who require much more support than what a general education teacher is able to provide in a class of 25–30 students. Some students may be able to do well with the support of a well-trained paraprofessional in a general education classroom, whereas other students require more intense support in the way of a specialized instructional program. Still other students may benefit most from a program that specializes in a particular type of support, whether it is support for emotional or behavioral needs, specific learning disabilities, or something else.

Mistake: Giving a stricter consequence to a student with a disability than a student without a disability

Solution: Before giving any consequence that involves suspension, police intervention, or removal of privileges, carefully check what school policy says would be the consequence for any student. Consider the previous example in which a student without a disability was provided a 5-day suspension because he brought drugs to school, but school personnel wanted to place a student with a disability in a 45-day interim alternative educational setting for the same offense. This cannot be done. If schools want to be proactive, then they need to establish policies for positive interventions, how students gain privileges, and the consequences for major infractions of school rules.

Removing educational field trips is one of the most common problems that occur. I received a call from a parent of a child with a disability protected under Section 504 because of reactive attachment disorder and ADHD. Her child was told that she could not go on a field trip because she had not behaved. My question was whether there was a set of behavior criteria for all students. It is permissible to have earned field trips for students who meet certain behavior criteria. Educational field trips that are a culmination of a classroom unit are different, however, and if the student participated in the unit and school personnel deny the field trip, then they are actually suspending the student for that period of time. An alternative would be to provide additional supervision for the field trip so the student could attend. These are difficult decisions to make because the safety of the group must be considered, but personnel should be careful that they are not denying an educational field trip because of the student's disability. Instead, they need to consider what accommodations could be made for the student to attend.

Mistake: Failure to monitor the number of suspension days that a student has received

Solution: Monitoring suspension days can be tough in large school districts in which there are multiple individuals in administration that may be able to suspend students. Also, if the teacher is not communicating with the district administrator about what he or she is doing, then it is extremely difficult to keep track of suspension days. One person needs to be designated to monitor discipline issues, specifically suspensions.

I saw an instance in which a student had been suspended for more than 20 days, and the building principal did not know this had happened until the parent filed a due process hearing. The teacher had been sending the student home for misbehavior without communicating what she was doing to the building principal. The student had also been suspended by the dean of students, and the principal had not been informed. Both of these incidents could have been prevented by better communication and by a specific designee that monitored any suspensions.

Mistake: Ignoring reports of bullying or turning the other way when students are bullied

Solution: All staff should be trained to report any incidents of bullying. I have observed adult playground supervisors allowing students to be bullied. School personnel who observe bullying must intervene right away and must report the incident to an official who is able to take action. If a student with a disability is involved with an incident of bullying, then the IEP team or 504 team must convene to determine the extent to which additional or different services are needed and ensure that needed changes are promptly made (U.S. Department of Education, 2014).

CHAPTER SUMMARY

As mandated by IDEA 2004, students with behavioral challenges resulting from a disability are entitled to appropriate supports and interventions so that they have access to a meaningful education. In order to improve student behavior, schools should move away from punitive disciplinary procedures, zero tolerance policies, and repeated suspensions to a tiered system of PBIS in which students are reinforced for positive behavior and behavioral issues are prevented through universal rules and expectations that are explicitly taught to all students. Students facing challenges not addressed by discipline policies and expectations for all students are provided with increasing levels of support, including special education services and a BIP if behavioral issues result from a disability and impede their ability to receive an education. First determine the function of the student's behavior when designing a BIP, and document this information through an FBA. This documentation is not only critical in understanding why the student behaves in a certain way but also in guiding how we should best intervene. Chapter 7 explores the importance of documentation for not only student behavior but also a multitude of day-to-day school-related activities.

Chapter 6 Extras and Activities

How to Advise? Tackling the Tough Questions in Special Education Law

Q: My child has been sent home for more than 20 days this year because he was disruptive in the classroom. I told the district that they could not suspend him that many days, but they told me that they were conducting a time-out and not a suspension by sending him home and, thus, were not limited by the number of days they could suspend him. Is sending a student home for the remainder of the day a suspension?

A: Yes, sending a student home for the remainder of a day, particularly if it is for the majority of the day, is considered a suspension. The student is being removed from the setting in which he is being educated and is not receiving an education during this time. This is not considered the appropriate use of time-out. Time-out is an extinction procedure in which the child is removed for a short period of time either in the classroom or outside the classroom. Time-out takes place at school so that the child is not completely removed from the learning environment and still has the ability to receive positive reinforcement.

Interact

- Get into a group of colleagues/fellow students and debate the following topic: "Suspension is an effective intervention."

- Form a group and develop criteria for using police intervention for students with challenging behaviors.

- Form a group and develop a flow chart that can be used for guidance on the appropriate use of the discipline requirements of IDEA 2004.

Online Activities

- In a discussion board, have an agree–disagree activity with fellow colleagues/students. The first person agrees with the statement: "Suspension is an effective intervention for students who engage in behavior problems." That person must justify why he or she agrees with the statement. The next person must disagree and justify his or her answer. The next person agrees, and so forth.

- *WebQuest:* Find one study that deals with using suspension as an intervention for students with challenging behaviors, and summarize the study in no more than five sentences.

How Many of These Acronyms Do You Know?*

There are many acronyms related to school discipline. Which of the following do you know?

FBA _____

BIP _____

PBIS _____

SWPBIS _____

ABC _____

Two Truths and a Lie*

Read all of these statements. Two are true, and one is a lie. Determine which one is a lie.

1. Students who bring weapons or drugs to school can be placed in an interim alternative educational setting for 45 school days.

2. Students can be suspended for 10 days at a time.

3. BIPs must be developed for those students with disabilities whose behavior interferes with their learning.

*Answers for activities noted with an asterisk are provided in the Answer Key for Extras and Activities appendix.

7

Understanding the Importance of Documentation

"If it isn't written down, it wasn't done." This is a motto that I utilize frequently to foster understanding that educators must document significant events in their work with students and their families. Word of mouth is simply not enough. It may sound harsh or even overly simple, but if an incident or intervention is not properly documented with date, time, people involved, and response or outcome, then it becomes difficult to prove that it happened. School personnel become busy and forget to write down important facts. For instance, an individual recording information during an IEP meeting does not record what was actually discussed. The special education teacher or the case manager fail to check the IEP for accuracy, and the teacher is held accountable when the IEP does not reflect the decision of the group. The IEP must reflect what is actually being done for the student. This chapter stresses the importance of documentation, explains what appropriate documentation is, and provides the basic rules to remember when documenting the variety of events that occur while working with students with disabilities.

As part of the documentation process, it is critical that educators do not tamper with information that is already in the student records. An article in the South Florida *Sun Sentinel* reported that some of the high school staff at a local school in the area fixed the grades of three football players (Shipley, 2014). Student transcripts were altered by certain staff members to allow the athletes to continue playing football. As a result of the violations, the school stripped access to student records from several employees and reset passwords for access to student records.

Although this case dealt with violations of academic records, it can also happen with IEPs. It is critical that team members are careful about their documentation, especially with web-based IEPs in which numerous individuals have access to those documents. They should not be changing information on an IEP without scheduling a new IEP meeting or seeking permission for an addendum to the IEP. Nothing should be changed on the IEP without the permission of the IEP team members, including the parents. Individuals may want to go into the IEP and add items after the meeting is over, but they cannot do so without consulting the entire team. Similarly, if a member of the IEP team wishes to include data such as additional test scores about the student prior to disseminating the IEP to participants, then that member must inform the other IEP team members and gain their permission. If such an action is not acceptable to all IEP team members, including the parents, then the data should be prepared and presented for the next IEP meeting for approval by the entire team.

If there is something in a record that you do not believe is accurate, then you should inform your administrator and the **records custodian** of that information. Remember that you must document the conversation with the administrator and records custodian in writing.

TYPES OF DOCUMENTATION

There are primarily three types of documentation that you will keep. The first type of documentation includes notes and logs that you will write about students as part of your classroom process. You are required to document attendance and progress in class. Many educators write down notes about students as it pertains to their behavior. Some teachers keep logs about students so they can read them later and determine whether there are trends in behavior. For example, a teacher might find that the student is more lethargic on Monday or that the student's absences seem to occur more on Wednesday. Such documentation can assist in targeting areas that require more attention. We get too close to a situation at times, and we cannot always see patterns in behavior unless we document what is occurring. We may be expected to document what students with medical needs eat each day or how many times they have to use the restroom. This information is valuable to you and others who may be working with the student. It is important that the documentation is objective and based on actual data, not personal opinions. It is also important to include the date and time of day so that when you return to the information after a period of time, you know exactly when it was written.

The second type of documentation involves recording communication with parents, colleagues, or community agencies. This documentation may include a parent telephone call. For example, a note goes home to a family about the IEP meeting that is to be held 3 weeks from today. That is followed up with a telephone call the following day. You should always document in writing the results of that telephone call, including the date of the call, time of the call, who you talked to, and what was said; then you should sign it. By doing so, you have proof that you made the telephone call. I recommend that you keep copies of forms for those calls by your desk so that it is easier for you to remember to complete the documentation. If you type a record of these calls on your computer, then remember to print and make copies to file. You should always keep a copy for yourself so that you have documented proof that you talked to the parent.

Recording interactions and communication with colleagues is another example of this second type of documentation. For example, a parent comes in to school and asks for a new evaluation of his child. You tell the parent that you will talk to the principal or special education supervisor about the request. You should then talk to the administrator, review the request, and send a follow-up in writing. You may want to write a note or letter to the principal that states, "As a follow-up to our conversation about (student)_____, his father came in to see me on (date)_____ and requested a new evaluation for his son. Please let me know the decision that is made about conducting the evaluation." Then remember to sign, date, and keep a copy of the documentation. This action protects you from someone stating that he or she did not know the parent asked for an evaluation. It is easy to forget to keep these kinds of records, but it is critical because this can save you problems in the future.

Finally, if you need to make a call to the Department of Children and Family Services or the Department of Health and Human Services for suspected abuse, neglect, or other issues, then you should always document in writing who you talked to, the date of the call, and a summary of the conversation. You may also need to coordinate with the school social worker or psychologist. Taking time to record information about these calls will assist you later in remembering the details about the situation. You also need to have proof that you made the call.

The third type of documentation is related to the IEP or other support plans that are part of the IEP, such as the BIP or a list of appropriate accommodations. For example, the IEP team may have determined the appropriate accommodations for the student on a statewide assessment. You are observing the student take the assessment with the accommodations and note that the student is easily distracted or that the student is putting his or her head down and taking a nap for the first hour of the test, even though he or she has been provided with the extended time line accommodation. You document the results of the accommodation in writing because this is valuable information for the IEP team. You may be working on a specific target behavior for the BIP and need to take baseline data without an intervention and then collect data and document results of the recommended intervention. This is information that is needed when the BIP is reviewed. You will also need to document in writing the results of formal and informal assessments of academic skills.

Some of the documentation will overlap or serve multiple purposes. Some of the general classroom information you collect may be useful for the IEP, and some parent contacts will be needed in the IEP. It is important to check documentation often for accuracy, precision, and objectivity.

BASIC PRINCIPLES OF THE LAWS AND REGULATIONS REGARDING DOCUMENTATION

This section presents some basic principles related to documentation; you can review the exact references cited in the federal regulations for a detailed description. In addition, you can review your state-specific laws and regulations, which are usually found on your state department's web site.

The **Family Educational Rights and Privacy Act (FERPA)** of 1974 (PL 93-380) is the law that governs the maintenance and release of records and explains the difference between permanent and temporary records. **Permanent records** consist of information such as high school transcripts, grades, and honors received. A permanent record is "maintained without time limitation." (34 C.F.R. 300.624). **Temporary records** are records that are kept for at least 5 years and consist of items such as special education evaluations, IEPs, and discipline records. References to special education services cannot go into the student's permanent record. School districts must provide the opportunity for a parent or eligible student to inspect and review the student's educational records. The school has to respond to reasonable requests for explanations and interpretations of records (FERPA regulations, 34 C.F.R. 99.10).

IDEA 2004 requires that the school district inform parents when personally identifiable information collected, maintained, or used is no longer needed to provide educational services to the child (34 C.F.R. 300.624). A permanent record of a student's name, address, and telephone number; his or her grades; attendance record; classes attended; grade level completed; and year completed may be maintained without time limitation.

Parental consent is required for evaluation, placement, and provision of special education services, and there must be appropriate documentation of that consent. Written parental consent must be obtained for an initial evaluation, and the school district must make reasonable efforts to obtain the informed consent. Likewise, the school system must make reasonable efforts to obtain informed consent for initial provision of services to the child. Finally, the school system must obtain informed consent for a reevaluation unless it has made reasonable efforts to obtain such consent and the parent has failed to respond (34 C.F.R. 300.300).

After a group of qualified professionals, including the parent of the child, has determined whether the child is a child with a disability, the school system must provide a copy of the evaluation report and documentation of determination of eligibility at no cost to the parent. Information to determine eligibility must be gained from a variety of sources and must be documented and carefully considered. An IEP must be developed if it is determined that the child is a child with a disability and needs special education (34 C.F.R. 300.306). Specific requirements are needed for documenting the determination of eligibility for a child suspected of having a specific learning disability, and each group member of the eligibility team must certify in writing whether the report reflects his or her conclusion about a learning disability. If it does not reflect a team member's conclusion, then that member must submit a separate statement that presents his or her conclusions (34 C.F.R. 300.311).

Written notice must be provided to parents whenever the school district proposes to initiate or change the identification, evaluation, or educational placement of the child or if the district refuses to begin or change one of these provisions. That notice must be in understandable language for the parents (34 C.F.R. 300.503). E-mail may be utilized if the school district makes that option available (34 C.F.R. 300.505). Parents must be notified of meetings early enough to ensure that they have the opportunity to attend, and those meetings are to be held at a mutually agreed-on time and place (34 C.F.R. 300.322). Schools must keep a record of attempts to arrange a mutually agreed-on time and place, such as detailed records of telephone calls or attempted telephone calls, copies of correspondence, or detailed records of visits to the home (34 C.F.R. 300.322).

This chapter's mnemonic provides strategies for maintaining consistent and accurate documentation as required by law.

Documentation may seem time consuming, but it should not be taken lightly and should never be an afterthought. This chapter's How Would You Rule? exercise imparts the seriousness of proper documentation and follow-up. In this case, a failure to monitor and accurately document a student's behavior is called into question after a student's death.

How Would You Rule?

A struggling middle school student died by suicide in 2007. The parent argued that the school district had suspicions that the young man had a disability. The student

Just 3 X 5 It: A Mnemonic to Help You Remember

Remember these key points to keep your documentation from being TOSSED.

T—Title: Always remember to put your specific title on the documentation you are providing.

O—Objective: Information in any type of incident report should be objective and not reflect an individual's opinion unless the information is documented as an opinion or the individual cites the source for the information.

S—Signature: Always sign any type of written communication and include your specific title and the date you wrote the document.

S—Share: Remember that a piece of information that is shared becomes part of the student's temporary record.

E—Evidence: Be sure that evidence-based information is contained in the documentation.

D—Date: Any documentation should contain the specific date and year.

had been absent frequently, had behavioral issues, and had faced repeated bullying by other students. The parent contended that these problems should have been documented and should have triggered an evaluation of the student. An evaluation was initiated 18 months after his behavioral issues began. The parent wanted to make a claim against the school district because of the suicide, and the parent claimed that the child had been denied a FAPE.

The student had been in special education at one time, but he exited the program 2 years before his suicide. The parent contended that the district did not conduct any formal evaluations or standardized tests and did not notify the parent before deciding that the student no longer needed services for students with learning disabilities. The district did eventually develop a 504 plan for the student because personnel believed he had ADHD. Would you rule in favor of the parent or the school district?

Your ruling:

_____
_____
_____
_____

The court's ruling:

The U.S. District Court ruled against the school district in *Scruggs v. Meriden Bd. of Educ.* (2007), stating that the student's absences and behavioral issues should have resulted in an evaluation. The parent was not notified that special education services had been discontinued, and the district developed a 504 plan without any medical confirmation of its suspicion that the student had ADHD. The plaintiff, the child's mother, successfully argued that the school district did not follow proper procedures in documenting and providing for her son's special education needs, did not adequately train staff, and did not execute appropriate antibullying and harassment policies (Cornell & Limber, 2015).

CASE STUDY COMPARISON

Proper documentation and communication between team members is lacking in the case of missteps and mistakes, resulting in a child who is not receiving needed services, a pair of dissatisfied parents, and a due process hearing. Contrast this with the exemplary approach in which careful, factual, and consistent documentation is part of an educator's daily routine. How do you think this kind of documentation benefits students and their families?

A Case of Missteps and Mistakes

Mrs. Jensen has been a resource special education teacher at Lincoln Elementary School for 10 years. She prides herself on being an excellent teacher and having a high degree of active engagement in her classroom. She also provides the necessary specialized instruction that her students need to succeed in school. She has difficulty delegating responsibilities, however, and likes to do most of the work herself. As a result, she often finds herself buried under a mound of paperwork. She just cannot seem to stay on top of it all. Her building principal has offered to have the office secretary schedule her IEP meetings, but she prefers doing this herself.

Mrs. Jensen knows that Billy's IEP is due, and she needs to get the meeting scheduled. She received a note in early September from Billy's mother, who was upset because Billy was not getting the speech-language services he should be receiving. Mrs. Jensen talked with the SLP at the beginning of the school year but did not document the conversation. In November, Billy is still not receiving speech-language services.

That same month, Mrs. Jensen finally asks the school secretary to mail the notice about the date and time for the meeting. She does not follow through to see whether the notice was actually sent. She then follows up via telephone to make sure that Billy's mother received the notice. Billy's mother claims she did not receive notice of the meeting. Mrs. Jensen tells her the date and time. Billy's mother tells Mrs. Jensen that she is upset that Billy is not receiving his speech-language services. Mrs. Jensen tells Billy's mother that she talked with the SLP at the beginning of the school year.

Mrs. Jensen calls Billy's mother the day before the IEP meeting to remind her about the meeting. She cannot reach her but does not worry—after all, she did tell her the date and time of the meeting once.

Neither Billy's mother nor father attends the IEP meeting. Mrs. Jensen tells the principal that it is okay to have the IEP meeting because three contacts were made with the mother. The principal voices concerns at the IEP meeting that he did not know that Billy was not receiving speech-language services, and he talks with the SLP and tells her that she must start seeing Billy as soon as possible. The IEP is then mailed to the mother.

The principal calls Mrs. Jensen in to the office at the end of the month, stating that he has received a request for a due process hearing from Billy's parents and their attorney. The issues listed in the dispute include failure to provide notice of an IEP meeting, failure to include the parent in the IEP process, and failure to provide speech-language services. Mrs. Jensen will need to meet with the school district's attorney to review the case.

On the day of the meeting between the school board attorney and Mrs. Jensen, the attorney questions Mrs. Jensen about why Billy is not receiving speech-language services. Mrs. Jensen explains that she talked with the SLP at the beginning of the year, but the SLP had a busy schedule, and there was a conflict with times to provide services. The attorney asks for documentation of her conversation with the SLP; Mrs. Jensen does not have any.

The attorney then asks about the written notice sent to the parents about the IEP meeting. Mrs. Jensen shows him a copy of the notice. There is no address on the notice. Mrs. Jensen then asks the secretary to what address the letter was sent. The secretary looked at the child's registration card and said she sent it to that address. Mrs. Jensen did not know that the secretary sent the notice to the wrong address. She reported that Billy told her his parents had moved, and she had a note from Billy's mother, but she had forgotten to tell the office that information. Mrs. Jensen reported to the attorney that she made two calls to the mother. When the attorney asked her for the written documentation of those efforts, Mrs. Jensen could not remember the exact dates.

What errors were made in this example? Consider the following list of missteps and mistakes:

- Mrs. Jensen failed to keep written records of her efforts to communicate with the SLP.

- Mrs. Jensen failed to communicate with the building principal that Billy was not receiving his speech-language services.

- Mrs. Jensen did not notify the office of the change of address.

- Although Mrs. Jensen did follow up with the parent on the telephone, she failed to document the telephone conversations in writing.

What could Mrs. Jensen have done to prevent this situation from occurring, and what can she do in the future?

- Mrs. Jensen needs to monitor the IEP on a continuous basis, and when she notices that the student is not receiving the services listed on the IEP, she should contact the person responsible for providing those services and then document that contact in writing.

- If the issue was not resolved after contacting the SLP, then Mrs. Jensen had the obligation to notify the principal that the student was not being provided speech-language therapy, and that conversation should have been documented in writing.

- Mrs. Jensen needs to have a talk (and follow up with a written communication) with the school secretary to let her know address changes, and she should keep a copy of the notification she received and written documentation about when it was shared with the office personnel.

- Mrs. Jensen could take a couple of actions to document contacts with parents. She could utilize the copy of the actual notice that was sent and could mark the following on that document: "Telephone contact made on 1-10-2016 at 3:15 P.M. by Mrs. Jensen to parent to remind her of the scheduled meeting." Mrs. Jensen could also create a standard form for parent conferences and complete the information regarding who, what, when, and where the follow-up contact was made.

The Exemplary Approach

Mr. George has been a special education teacher of students with emotional and behavior disorders for more than 15 years. He has learned how important documentation is when working with students with behavioral challenges. He documents the behaviors of his students so he can look for patterns and can keep the parents and his administration informed of changes in his students' behaviors. Mr. George refrains from subjective statements such as, "Bill just won't do his work," when he is documenting behavior. Instead he makes statements such as, "Bill has not completed his independent math assignments at the fourth-grade level three out of five times." He keeps his documentation as objective and as precise as possible. He may put a week's worth of a student's behavioral logs on one page, but he provides the date and time of the day that the incident occurred on each entry of the log and the time and date that he wrote the entry. He signs the bottom of each page of the log along with his position. This is important because pages may get separated. He retains these logs in the files that he has for each student.

Mr. George has learned the importance of logging both positive behaviors and behaviors of concern so that he can share that information with the family and his administration. He is prepared with the necessary factual information when he attends an IEP meeting for one of his students.

SOLUTIONS TO COMMON MISTAKES

The following are common mistakes that are made concerning documentation and possible solutions to those problems.

Mistake: Failure to record behavior incidents. Identifying patterns of behavioral concerns exhibited by students is critical in today's schools. A student makes a threat, a student gets in a fight on the playground, a student gets caught inappropriately touching another student—these occurrences need to be recorded. I worked with many schools dealing with children with challenging behaviors and learned that school personnel would call when a major incident occurred in the school. I would ask whether there had been any previous problems, and many would respond that there had been, but it was an isolated incident. I would go to the school to interview various individuals, however, and I would learn that previous behavior incidents had occurred, but they were only stored in memory. No one recorded the incidents in writing.

School personnel are reluctant to write up behavior incidents at times because they do not want to prejudice other school personnel or a new school about a student. The individuals who are working with the student, however, have a right to know that the student has behavioral concerns. We have all read about tragic incidents that occurred within schools; in those instances, people came forward after the fact to relay critical pieces of information that a number of individuals knew about but failed to record and act on to help the student.

School personnel may send a student home for the remainder of the day after a behavior incident, and no written record of this action is made. Perhaps the assistant principal or dean sent the student home and did not record the information. A major incident occurs, and the principal makes the decision to suspend the student for 10 days; the parent disputes the suspension, saying that the student has been suspended at least 25 days during the year. The principal does not realize this because the school has no written documentation of sending the students home; however, the parents have their documentation.

Solution: When a student engages in a behavior that warrants action, the incident should be recorded with the date, time, and signature of the individual who witnessed the event. The recording of the incident should be objective. This documentation establishes a pattern of behavior, signaling that the student needs assistance. The administrator may have students sent to the office repeatedly—that information should be documented. The administrator should also be proactive with the teacher and find out what is occurring within the classroom. The administrator should require the teacher to document behavior incidents so the administrator can review the information with the teacher and provide assistance. Expecting the teacher to document such an incident may deter the teacher from quickly sending the student to the office, and, even if it does not, it provides the administrator with the necessary documentation to help the student and assist the teacher in working with the student.

Mistake: Failure to provide written notice to parents, document contact with parents, and keep copies of all contacts. The law is very specific about the required notices that must be sent to parents. Copies of all contacts with parents should be kept, whether written or by telephone. School personnel tend to be conscientious about the written notices that are sent to parents, but may not check for a correct address or do not always get the notice out in a timely manner. Follow-up telephone calls also may not be documented.

Solution: Having provided notices of thousands of IEP meetings during my career, I learned to always keep parent conference forms readily available at my desk. Any time I called a parent or a parent called me or visited the school, I would write a summary of the conference, date it, sign it, and make a copy for my files and the special education file. I always made the effort to document the call right after I had talked with the parent. Otherwise, significant information may not be recalled.

Mistake: Failure to include all necessary information in any documentation, including date and all pertinent details

Solution: Check all written documentation to make sure that it has the date and all objective information. Written documentation should be signed and dated by the individual who authored it. The dates can be different because the incident may have occurred on one day, but the actual documentation did not take place until the following day. The author of the documentation must also document his or her position or job title, such as special education teacher, occupational therapist, or SLP.

Mistake: Failure to write the decisions that were made by the IEP team on the IEP document

Solution: Records must be portable, meaning that when a student moves or school personnel change, new personnel at either the new school or the current school must understand what the IEP document states. The IEP should clearly reflect the achievement and developmental levels of the student, the goals for the student, and the placement recommendations.

The individual recording the IEP must review what is written down to make sure that there is clarity and that an individual who did not know the student prior to a placement would be able to pick the document up and know exactly what the student needs. For example, if co-teaching with a special education teacher within the general education classroom is recommended, then it should be clearly delineated on the IEP.

Recorders will write in shorthand at times, stating that the child spends "five periods per day in the general education classroom." They do not specify that there is a co-teacher who is a special educator in the classroom. The student then moves to another school district, and new personnel assume that the student spends the majority of his or her day in a general education classroom. They do not have a clue that a special education teacher is there all of the time. That is significant information that can make a big difference in the programming for the child.

Precisely record what is discussed at the IEP meeting as well as final decisions that are made. The recorder should review the document at the end of the IEP meeting to see whether everything that was discussed was recorded.

Mistake: All the participants come to the meeting and sign in that they are present, but one of the participants who signed in at the beginning of the IEP team meeting gets called out within 5 minutes by the school secretary to deal with a problem within the classroom. Although the participant had every intention of staying through the entire meeting, the problem requires about 40 minutes of his or her time, and the meeting is concluding by the time he or she returns. The participant was not there for the meeting, yet he or she had signed in that he or she was present.

Solution: When an individual documents that he or she is a participant in the IEP, the individual is agreeing to participate in the entire meeting. If the special education teacher gets called out for a crisis, then it may be necessary to recess the meeting until the teacher can return because the special education teacher is a required participant in the process.

Mistake: Failure to be objective when documenting information. It is important to remember that the parent or student will have access to their educational records, and special education teachers should not write anything down that they do not want reviewed by anyone else. All educational personnel are accountable for all written information and must be prepared to defend that information. Information that is not grounded in factual data should be avoided.

Solution: Do not record information that is hearsay or is an opinion that could be construed as judgmental. If information being documented is second-hand information, then the source for the documentation must be given.

Mistake: Failure to document any incident as soon as possible after it occurs. Educators are busy, and it is easy to forget the details of the incident unless it is written down as quickly as possible.

Solution: Start the incident report or record the results of a parent contact as soon as possible after the event occurs. This helps teachers remember to finish the report when they have a spare minute. Work to complete the form by the end of the school day. The longer teachers wait to write the details about an incident, the more likely they are to forget some of those details.

Mistake: Documentation of information about special education in the permanent record of the student

Solution: Special education records are part of the student's temporary record and should not be included in the student's permanent record. No reference to special education can appear in the permanent file of the student, so periodically check the records to ensure that no mention of special education is on the student's transcript.

Mistake: Destruction of documentation that is necessary to plan an appropriate educational program for the student

Solution: IDEA 2004 provides for the destruction of records. Parents must be notified when personally identifiable information is no longer needed to provide educational services to the child. The individual who is designated as the records custodian is responsible for periodically reviewing files to see what information is still pertinent to the child's education. All special educators should work closely with that individual to ascertain what information should be kept.

CHAPTER SUMMARY

This chapter discussed the importance of consistently maintaining factual, precise, and timely documentation of our work with students with disabilities, whether we are documenting important discussions and decisions on the IEP, our communication with colleagues and parents, the child's attendance and overall progress, or a behavior incident or instance of bullying. The following chapter takes a closer look at student records and issues of student confidentiality in record keeping and interacting with colleagues.

Chapter 7 Extras and Activities

How to Advise? Tackling the Tough Questions in Special Education Law

Q: I am a special education teacher at the secondary level. I recently was asked by one of my former students, now 19 years of age, for a copy of the discipline notes I kept about him. Do I have to give him that information?

A: If the temporary records of the student are available, and they should be because the student has only been out of school for a few years, then the student does have the right to his temporary records, which includes his discipline records.

Apply Your Knowledge

1. Get into a group and play a This or That activity. Put two signs up at either side of the room. Put a sign up that says "This" on one side of the room. Put a sign up that says "That" on the other side of the room. "This" denotes permanent records. "That" denotes temporary records. Read the following phrases, and have participants move to the sign indicating which type of record contains that information.

    *   Grades

    *   Special education evaluations

    *   504 plan

    *   List of medications a student is taking

    *   Basic identifying information such as birth date

    *   Sports played

    *   Special education classes taken

2. Determine whether these statements are subjective or objective statements.

    *   Bill is poorly motivated

    *   John refuses to do math

    *   Gratia is manipulating

    *   Javez is argumentative

    *   Marie's parents are difficult to work with

    After critiquing these statements, rewrite the statements in objective terms

Interact

*   Prepare a skit with a partner to present to fellow colleagues/students. You and your partner are disagreeing about a subject and start raising your voices. One participant then pushes the other. Have the audience write their impression of what happened in three sentences. Then, have several audience members

volunteer to read what they have written. Explain how observations often vary and may not always be objective.

- If this is an in-service activity, then go around the room and interview 10 colleagues to see if they can name the records custodian for their building. If this is a preservice activity, then interview five teachers to see if they know their school's records custodian.

Online Activities

- Go online and find a story about an incident in a school with a student. Review the story and count the number of subjective comments that were made.

- Go online and locate the FERPA regulations. Then, find three facts that you did not know about FERPA.

Two Truths and a Lie*

Read all of these statements. Two are true, and one is a lie. Determine which one is a lie.

1. A student's attendance records are part of his or her permanent records.

2. A student's discipline records are part of his or her permanent records.

3. All schools have to have an individual designated as a records custodian.

*Answers for activities noted with an asterisk are provided in the Answer Key for Extras and Activities appendix.

8

The Rules of
Record Keeping
and Confidentiality

This chapter focuses on three areas—what constitutes a record, the handling of records, and the important role of the records custodian. Second, this chapter defines who can gain access to records and who needs to know specific information about a student. Information about publicly posting certain details of individual student performance is included in this section. Third, this chapter discusses our role as confidential employees and describes with whom we can share specific information.

STUDENT RECORDS

What constitutes a record? A record is anything recorded by hand, digitally, or by audio means that is shared with another individual. For example, some teachers keep a notebook as an informal log to track a student's progress every day. They may do so because they are looking for patterns in behavior or academic regression. This information is private unless it is shared either verbally or in writing with anyone else. Once it is shared in any way, it becomes a part of the student record. Yet, if a social worker is told information privately by a student in a one-to-one session and records that information but never shares it with anyone else (as long as that information will not cause harm to the student or another person), then it does not become part of the record. Remember that all reports, data, and correspondence must be factual, signed, and dated, noting the person's current job title.

There are two types of records according to FERPA. Permanent records are those records that stay on file at a school and are "maintained without time limitation." (34 C.F.R. 300.624). Permanent records consist of general information about the student (e.g., student's name and date of birth, high school transcript, grades, extracurricular activities), whereas temporary records are kept at least 5 years and contain information related to special education services (e.g., evaluations, IEPs) and discipline. A student has the right to his or her own records when he or she exits the school system, and the school system must notify the student and family that these records are available.

Records must be kept and cannot be destroyed unilaterally. The Institute for Education Sciences has posted helpful information about the handling of records at http://nces.ed.gov/pubs97/web/97859.asp. States also have specific laws and regulations that govern procedures for what happens when a parent wants specific records destroyed or altered. It is up to each state to determine how to conduct a records hearing. School personnel can learn about their own state's procedures for conducting a records hearing at the appropriate state department of education's web site, which is a site that all school personnel should become familiar with to stay current with state-specific information.

ISSUES OF CONFIDENTIALITY

Who can access student records, and who has the need to know? In many cases, school personnel are afraid to share certain information with other people within the school because they fear they will be accused of violating confidentiality laws. The key question to ask is, "Does the individual have the right to know?" If the individual does, then the information should be shared. For example, the student may have a seizure disorder and is transported on the bus. The bus driver needs to know this information and should be trained on procedures that must be followed if the student has a seizure while being transported. The cafeteria workers should be informed if a student who comes through the lunch line has specific food allergies. If a student is in a special education program and has a criminal record, then the special education teacher needs to know. If the parent of a student is a convicted sex offender, then the principal and any of the staff with whom the student interacts have a right to know because there are specific laws in some states that govern whether those individuals are able to come into the school. The school district has the obligation to train relevant staff on confidentiality laws when such sensitive and personal information is being disclosed. The school administrator(s) will determine who needs to know what information. Certainly, members of the IEP team will need to know about the specific needs of the student, as well as other staff members interacting with the student. Simply put, any adult within the school system who is working with a student should be informed about specific characteristics related to the student's disability.

A common question that arises is whether students should be told about other classmates' disabilities. This is best determined on a case-by-case basis, but always proceed with utmost caution about this and discuss this with the student and/ or the parents before anything is disclosed to other students. Some families may prefer to keep information private, whereas others might take the opportunity to teach other students about a disability or specific health condition. Should the family decide to share personal information, it is best to have the parent or the student disclose this information rather than school staff.

Parents have the right to inspect records and have a copy of the records. The student has the right to the records when he or she has reached the age of majority, according to the state's definition. Schools serve as the custodian of records, which rightfully belong to the parent and the student.

Each school is responsible for designating an individual who is the records custodian, and it is critical that all staff are informed of that individual. The records custodian may be a school secretary, the school principal, or someone else designated by the school administration. Whenever there is a question about records, school staff should submit a request for records to that individual. One person is designated as the records custodian in most school systems. That individual must be trained on confidentiality laws, how record requests are handled, and what is done when someone wants records destroyed. All school districts must develop specific policies and procedures concerning records. All staff need to be given copies of those policies and procedures and are expected to follow them. Records custodians should keep a record of who has viewed the records and when those records have been reviewed.

With the increased utilization of online IEPs, it is important that school personnel ensure that only predetermined, authorized personnel with the right to know have access to the IEP online. Many of today's dangers are related to unauthorized access to online records, and schools must make every possible effort to have a secure online system for storage and access to all student records, including IEPs. They should also have a mechanism in place in which the use of those systems is periodically monitored to see who is gaining access to a child's IEP.

All educators must understand their professional responsibility to maintain both student and co-worker confidentiality. This means that they must be careful to avoid traps inside and outside their school building that result in sharing information with individuals who do not have a need to know. For example, a relative of a child may work in the school district and want access to information about the student, but the relative does not have a right to know about confidential information unless he or she is the legal guardian. Teachers' lounges are places where teachers may need to vent, but they cannot share confidential information about students. All educators have to monitor their behavior to make sure they are not sharing information that should not be shared. They should not be talking about students or colleagues outside the school setting where someone can overhear what they say. You may be familiar with a student's extended family, but it is not okay to discuss a student's progress when you run into his or her aunt at the grocery store because his or her aunt is not the legal guardian. Similarly, you may run into the mother of one of your students in the pharmacy, and it would be tempting to update her on her daughter's progress. Other individuals in the pharmacy may overhear the conversation. Sharing information with friends outside the school setting is similarly inappropriate. A teacher might send an e-mail to a friend about a student in a moment of frustration, and he or she might even mention the name of the student. The teacher violated that student's right to privacy by electronically sharing information with a friend who does not need to have the information.

Confidentiality not only applies to personal information about students but also to co-workers and staff. Perhaps one teacher shared medical information with another teacher in confidence, or shared other personal information, but it was not meant to be shared. It is natural to develop close relationships and share personal information because school staff spend so much time together, but care must be taken with those details. It is inappropriate to share personal information, regardless of how the faculty member learned the information.

Being contacted about a professional reference for an individual applying for a promotion or new job is another dilemma an educator might face. Someone may call you and state that he or she is doing a reference check on a person that you may or may not have written a reference about. You do not know whether the individual is actually the person he or she claims to be, however, or whether that individual is just checking you out to see what you will say. It is best to ask for the individual's name and telephone number when in doubt, and tell the person you will call him or her back. That way, you can verify the person's actual identity.

Finally, a word about social media. Social media is a wonderful means of communicating and keeping track of friends and family, but anything posted online via Facebook, Instagram, Twitter, or any other social media platform is there for the world to see, and once something is posted, it is next to impossible for it to be removed. Whether you had a bad day with colleagues or a supervisor, you disagree with a co-worker's view, or a student just pushed you past your breaking point, be aware that whatever gets posted online can end up hurting yourself or others. Moreover, we need to build up our profession rather than making comments that are destructive.

Public school district employees must remember that they are public servants and responsible to the public for their actions. School employees are role models for students and members of their community. Inappropriate activity on social media is very problematic and can cause serious damage to a person's reputation, with the risk of suspension or even termination of employment. Of course, educators are entitled to a life outside of school, but carefully consider what is said in public forums such as Facebook because your actions could have serious, negative effects for you or your colleagues.

BASIC PRINCIPLES OF THE LAWS AND REGULATIONS REGARDING RECORD KEEPING AND CONFIDENTIALITY

Guidance for handling data and personal information is found in IDEA 2004 and FERPA. According to FERPA, educational records are directly related to a student and maintained by an educational agency or institution or by a party acting for the agency or institution. "*Record* means any information recorded in any way, including, but not limited to, handwriting, print, computer media, video or audio tape, film, microfilm, and microfiche" (20 U.S.C. 1232g and 34 C.F.R. Part 99.3). The term does not include records of the law enforcement unit of an educational agency, and it does not include records that are kept in the sole possession of the maker, are used only as a personal memory aid, and are not accessible or revealed to any other person except a temporary substitute for the maker of the record (20 U.S.C. 1232g and 34 C.F.R. Part 99).

Disclosure means to permit access to records and refers to the release, transfer, or other communication of personally identifiable information contained in education records by any means (e.g., oral, written, electronic) to any party except the person that is identified as the individual that provided or created the record. "*Disclosure* means to permit access to or the release, transfer, or other communication of personally identifiable information contained in education records by any means, including oral, written, or electronic means, to any party except the party identified as the party that provided or created the record" (C.F.R. Part 99.3). It is necessary to gain prior written consent to release information to any other party than to another public school where the student will be attending, and the consent must include the specific records to be disclosed, the purpose of the disclosure, and the party to which the disclosure is being made (20 U.S.C. 1232g and 34 C.F.R. 99). "The parent or eligible student shall provide a signed and dated written consent before an educational agency or institution discloses personally identifiable information from the students' education records. . . ." (34 C.F.R. 99.30). Records can be released without consent to the following parties and for the following purposes:

1. To school officials within the school system who have been determined to have legitimate educational interests

2. To other public school officials in a school to which the student seeks or intends to enroll, provided the parent has been notified

3. To appropriate parties in connection with financial aid for which the student has applied

4. To state and local authorities pursuant to a state statute concerning the juvenile justice system and the system's ability to serve the student

5. To an organization conducting studies for, or on behalf of, educational agencies and institutions for the purposes of developing, validating, or administering predictive tests; administering student aid programs; or improving instruction

6. To accrediting organizations

7. To the parents of an eligible student if the student is a dependent student according to the Internal Revenue Service

8. To appropriate parties in connection with a health or safety emergency. FERPA does provide that "An educational agency or institution may disclose personally identifiable information from an education record to appropriate parties, including parents of an eligible student, in connection with an emergency if knowledge of the information is necessary to protect the health or safety of the student or other individuals." (34 C.F.R. 99.36)

9. To the eligible student

10. For the purpose of complying with a judicial order or subpoena

11. For the purpose of serving as directory information provided the school gave public notice of the types of information it has designated as directory information (20 U.S.C. 1232g and 34 C.F.R. 99)

Records cannot be shared with other agencies or private schools unless the parents have specifically signed for the release of those records. **Written parental consent for the release of information** must be signed and dated and must specify the records to be disclosed, state the purpose of the disclosure, and identify the party or class of parties to whom the disclosure may be made (FERPA and 34 C.F.R. 99).

   Access rights refer to the parents' right to have copies of the records. **Parent right to review records** refers to the parents' ability to review all school records, both temporary and permanent, and receive a copy of those records. Each school district "must permit parents to inspect and review any education records relating to their children that are collected, maintained, or used by the agency under this part" (34 C.F.R. 300.613)." Parents also have the right to have copies of the records containing the information (34 C.F.R. 300.613). "The agency must comply with a request for records without unnecessary delay and before any meeting regarding an IEP, or any hearing. . . ." (34 C.F.R. 300.613). The school does have the right to charge a fee for copying the records if the fee does not effectively prevent the parents from exercising their right to inspect and review the records (34 C.F.R. 300.617). Parents are able to request amendments to the information contained in records, and the school must decide whether to amend. If the school refuses to do so, then the parents must be notified and advised that they have the right to a records hearing.

The Health Insurance Portability and Accountability Act (HIPAA) of 1996 (PL 104-191) protects the privacy of individually identifiable health information (www.hhs.gov/hipaa/index.html). Many instances occur in which health information is included in a student's temporary record. The student may have been diagnosed with ADHD, obsessive compulsive disorder, or diabetes by a physician, and that information may be included in a health history or a psychological report. Rules discuss what information is protected and how protected health information can be utilized and disclosed. It is important to be aware of these rules and to carefully follow them when dealing with private health information.

This chapter's mnemonic is a summary and reminder of critical points related to confidentiality and record keeping.

The following How Would You Rule? exercise deals with the disclosure of a student's educational records. Apply what you know about the family's right to educational data to the following case.

Just 3 X 5 It: A Mnemonic to Help You Remember

Be very CAREFUL when observing confidentiality laws to protect the privacy of students and families.

C—Confidential treatment of records is critical.

A—Amending records is possible but only under certain conditions.

R—Records are of two types: temporary and permanent.

E—Emergency release of records for health or safety reasons is allowed under certain conditions.

F—Family Educational Rights and Privacy Act (FERPA) of 1974 (PL 93-380) is the federal law that protects the records of students.

U—Understanding the laws and rules about records is important because you must be able to explain the records to the parent.

L—Legal guardian of the student has the right to review the records.

How Would You Rule?

In this case, parents requested educational testing data. Specifically, the parents requested documentation completed by school district personnel concerning RTI, an approach considered by the entire IEP team. The district had implemented an RTI plan as an intermediate step before referring a child to special education. The district conducted universal assessments and then discussed those assessment results. The student received a variety of reading interventions in kindergarten and first grade through RTI.

The parents made a written request in October of the child's first-grade year that the child be evaluated to determine whether he had a learning disability. An additional two student study team meetings were held with the parents in November and February. The student study teams consisted of the student's teachers, the building administrator, and the school social worker. The RTI data graphs were not reviewed during those meetings. The district conducted the evaluation in March and April 2007 and determined the child's eligibility for special education services, diagnosing him with specific learning disabilities. They then held an IEP meeting whereby it was determined that the student would participate in the school's instructional support program for 45 minutes a day for 4 days a week. An annual review was held in March 2008, and the same services were offered. The parents got a private evaluation and paid for their son to attend sound-based therapy. The district convened another IEP team meeting in September 2008, and the parents voiced their concern about their son's lack of progress. The parents then requested an independent evaluation. The district did not respond to that request and sought the parents' consent to reevaluate the child. The parents got an independent evaluation, which found that the child had auditory processing weaknesses and severe dyslexia. Did the parents have the right to gain access to the RTI data that was collected by the district?

Your ruling:

_____

_____

_____

_____

The court's ruling:

In this case, *M.M. v. Lafayette School Dist., 767 F. 3d 842-Court of Appeals, 9th Circuit 2014, (64 Individuals with Disabilities Law Report, 31)*, the school district violated IDEA 2004's procedural requirements by failing to provide the parents with the RTI data. The district utilized the RTI data to corroborate the 2007 assessment that determined services for the child. The district did violate IDEA 2004 by failing to ensure that the RTI data was documented and carefully considered by the entire IEP team and failing to supply the parents with the data.

CASE STUDY COMPARISON

The following case studies deal with confidentiality breaches within the school system. A school staff member in the first example discusses a student in a public place and violates the student's privacy, leading to repercussions for the individual in question. In contrast, school personnel in the exemplary case study are properly trained on issues related to record keeping and confidentiality. Read and contrast these scenarios to learn solutions and safeguards for ensuring that every student's privacy is protected.

A Case of Missteps and Mistakes

It has been a long week at Riverside Middle School, and the long-awaited bell rings, marking a highly anticipated 3-day weekend. Many teachers, the school social worker, the school psychologist, and other staff members often go out socially before a break, but this week it is a smaller group because many people have travel plans. So, the social worker and two teachers, eager to unwind, go out to one of the local bars, where they find themselves in a booth with high backs. They fail to notice who is sitting in the booth behind them.

They start hashing over the events of the week and begin talking about all of the behavior problems that one student, Andy, has been having. The social worker shares with the teachers that Andy's father and mother are getting a divorce, and Andy is taking it hard. She makes it clear that this does not give him the right to act like a jerk. The social worker comments to the teachers in a low tone of voice, "Well, you know Andy has bipolar disorder, just like his mother." The two teachers are shocked. One of them exclaims in a louder tone of voice, "Oh, my gosh. I did not know that Andy was bipolar!" They finish their drinks, pay the bill, and head out the door.

The principal calls the social worker into the office on Tuesday morning when school resumes and asks her if she was at Eddie's Bar on Friday evening. The social worker offers that she was there with two of the teachers. The principal explains that Andy's aunt and uncle overheard the conversation in which the social worker shared that Andy was bipolar and having a lot of behavior problems at school and that Andy's mother also has bipolar disorder. The social worker apologizes. The principal tells her that her apology is not enough; Andy's family is requesting a disciplinary hearing for the social worker. The social worker is shocked; she did not realize that anyone heard her but the teachers to whom she was talking.

What errors were made in this example? Consider the following lists of missteps and mistakes:

- Never talk about students in a public place where there is the possibility that someone will hear the conversation. The social worker and teachers thought it was okay to mention a student's name because they only used a first name. It can be all too easy to identify a child, however, even when only a first name is used.

    I can remember going to a conference out of state and overhearing two teachers who were talking about a student who had moved from one district to another. They were standing by me and did not think that I would know the student, whom they referred to by first and last name. There is no way they could have been sure I did not know the student. Such public discussions of a student in proximity to other individuals who have no need to know about the child is a violation of FERPA.

What could be done in the future to prevent this from reoccurring?

- The staff should avoid drinking in a bar after school if they want to debrief about the school week. It is too easy to get a loose tongue and start discussing students when one is drinking.

- If the group wants to go out after school, then they should establish a clear rule that they will not talk about students or staff within the school. Staff at school should never discuss the school week in a public place.

The Exemplary Approach

Mr. Johns is the new principal of Alvarez Junior High School. He is taking over this position as a result of several breaches of confidentiality from at least three staff members and the principal that occurred within the school district last year. Those breaches resulted in the previous principal resigning from his position. Mr. Johns begins his new position with a proactive and positive approach. He does not want to point fingers about what happened in the past. Instead, he believes that he must accept responsibility to make changes. He meets with the records custodian and the secretary before school starts to review policies and procedures regarding records. He observes that these policies and procedures are in place and are in accord with FERPA and state law. The problem appears to be that these policies were not followed.

Mr. Johns plans a day of training on the laws and regulations governing information about students as a part of staff development days. He reviews the latest changes in FERPA and its accompanying regulations. He also prepares a series of scenarios (not related to anything that happened in the past) in which staff work together in small groups to talk about how they would handle these situations. He then talks about the positive expectations of the staff concerning records and confidentiality about students and staff. He lets staff know that he wants to work together with them through an open-door policy to deal with any questions they have about these issues.

Mr. Johns works closely with the staff throughout the school year, reviewing policies and procedures on confidentiality. He works with the staff to resolve any questions about records, confidentiality, or legal issues.

Because all of the staff now know the expectations and know that Mr. Johns wants to work collaboratively, a violation of records laws only occurs once with a particular staff member, and Mr. Johns works directly with that individual to resolve the issue as quickly as possible.

SOLUTIONS TO COMMON MISTAKES

Following are some further common mistakes made in regard to record keeping and confidentiality, with accompanying solutions.

Mistake: You mark on the student's report card that his math class is in special education and his grade is based on a modified grading system.

Solution: The report card can be part of the permanent record and, therefore, should not note any mention of special education or a modified grading system if a modified grading system is only utilized for special education students.

Nothing that denotes special education should be reflected in a permanent record.

Mistake: The parent comes to the school and wants the records of the student right away. You refuse to give the parent the records.

Solution: You should refer the parents to the records custodian, who is the individual that handles any requests for records. Although the parent does have the right to inspect the records and receive a copy of those records, the parent cannot come in and demand records immediately. It will take awhile for the records custodian to gather the records and get them ready for copying.

The records custodian should ensure that someone is in the room with the parent when he or she is reviewing the records in case there are questions or the parent removes records from the files unbeknownst to the school district personnel.

The school district does have the right to charge parents a reasonable fee for copying the records. Many school districts do not do this unless the files are large. They see it as a goodwill gesture to provide the parents with at least one set of the records.

Mistake: One of your students is in an extracurricular club that only consists of special education students. You note this on the student's transcript.

Solution: If it is known that the extracurricular club only consists of special education students, then this should not appear in the student's transcript because there should be no mention of special education in a transcript, which is a permanent record. School personnel could make sure that the club is open to non–special education students, however, and that there is nothing in the title of the club that denotes special education. The club could then be listed on the transcript.

Mistake: The records for one of your students are now in two expanding files. You have limited file space and decide that you will go through the files and throw away material that you do not believe is important anymore.

Solution: You may go through the student's records and see if there are examples of work that the student has done. You can then check with the school's record custodian and the principal to make sure it is permissible to give the parent a copy of this work. If so, then give the work to the parent or the student, depending on his or her age, and make a notation in the file that you have given samples of the student's work between the dates of "x" and "y." Have the parent sign that he or she has received the information from you, and then enter that paper into the student's record. Other records for the student should not be removed until the student has exited the school system, and the removal or discarding of any materials in the record should meet the requirements of your specific school district.

Mistake: A student of yours has told you that he intends to blow up the school building. You do not tell anyone because you do not want to violate the student's right to privacy.

Solution: You must tell someone when there is the possibility that the student could do damage to the building and other students and staff. FERPA states that you have a legal obligation to report what you have heard when there is danger involved and a student tells you such information. In many real cases in which there has been harm to others, the student had displayed warning signs and told someone information that should have been shared and could have prevented the deaths of individuals.

Mistake: A student tells you that his or her mother is sexually abusing him or her. You do not believe that he or she is telling the truth, so you decide to take no action.

Solution: When we are informed of potential abuse or harm to a child, it is not our job to determine whether the allegation is serious. It is our job to report the incident to the appropriate child welfare agency and let them determine the truth of the report and what action should be taken. A serious concern that I have heard encountered over a number of years is that the educator does not make a report of abuse because he or she does not believe the child welfare agency will do anything about it. Like any institution, the child welfare system may have its flaws, but we cannot use this type of reasoning as an excuse to not report an incident; we must always fulfill our responsibilities as mandated reporters and let the agency do its job. If we believe that the child welfare agency will do nothing, then when we make the call, we should ask for the name of the individual who has answered the telephone and write down specifically what that individual says. Tell the individual that you are documenting the call and then document the call, the date, the individual who took the call, and what you reported to the individual.

In one of the saddest cases I was involved in related to child sexual abuse, a child reported to one of my colleagues that he had been sexually abused several different times. Each time the student confided in my colleague, she reported the incident. She documented each call in writing with the time, the date, the person she talked to, and a summary of the conversation. One day, there was an incident of such serious sexual abuse that the student had obvious health problems as a result and ended up at a doctor's office. The doctor reported the situation, and the child was removed from the home.

The parent tried to get the student back home, and, as a result, a hearing was conducted. My colleague attended the hearing. The judge listened to the facts of the case. The judge then asked the child welfare agency whether it had any previous reports before the doctor reported the sexual abuse. The child welfare agency reported that the doctor's report was the first report it had ever received. Luckily, my colleague had documentation to back her up. She spoke of all the records she had kept, recounting each time she had made a call to the child welfare agency and thoroughly explaining each conversation, naming the worker with whom she talked and what that individual said. She summarized a total of eight reports she had made. The judge was appalled, ordered the child removed from the parent's home, and reprimanded the child welfare agency for its lack of action on behalf of this child. In this case, proper reporting and repeated documentation was crucial in helping a child in danger.

Mistake: Someone calls you and tells you that he or she is the student's parent. That individual asks you for information about the student. You may never have talked to this parent before, or you are not sure that the voice on the other end is actually the parent. You give out information over the telephone and later find out that the individual was not who he said he was. I have had students call and try to disguise their voice to pretend like they are one of their parents.

Solution: Be cautious when giving any information out over the telephone. When in doubt, write the telephone number down and tell the person that you will call him or her back. Verify that the telephone number actually belongs to the parent. You may want to elicit the support of someone who knows the voice of the parent or who is familiar with the parent. For example, the school social worker may know the parent and can verify the number and the parent's voice.

Mistake: You run into Johnny's grandma or aunt in the grocery store. You know them and stop to chat. They ask you questions about Johnny. You give them information.

Solution: This happens often, particularly in small communities where many people know each other. Yet, we must honor the confidentiality of the student and the student's family. Imagine if you gave out information to the aunt or uncle that you have not provided to the parent. The relative goes to the parent and shares the information. You have severed any relationship you may have had with the parent and have clearly violated confidentiality laws. When a relative asks for information, you need to reply, "I am sorry, but I cannot share any information with you. How have you been?" You should then change the subject. By making such a comment, you show that you do not spread student information to anyone who does not have a right to know and yet have been polite in your response. Unless the aunt, uncle, or grandparent is the legal guardian of the student, they do not have the right to the information.

Be sure to know the student's legal guardian. Communicate with the building administrator to see who is listed as the guardian. Different states have different laws and regulations for determining who the legal guardian is and the rights of custodial and noncustodial parents.

Mistake: You are upset and send an e-mail to your friends about what one of your students did today. You are not concerned because you did not mention the student by name.

Solution: It is never a good idea to air such information electronically. You may have sent the information to someone who is a friend or relative of the student's mother, and the individual clearly knows who the student is that you are mentioning. Although e-mail appears to be a great way to communicate, we must be very careful because e-mails become part of the student's record. It is also easy for someone to mean to respond to one person and instead click "reply to all," sending information out to people who have no need to have the information.

Mistake: You post derogatory comments on Facebook about the kind of day you had at school. You might say, "Wow, I had a rough IEP today with a very difficult parent," or, "One of my students was a pain in the butt today."

Solution: Avoid making any negative comments about your position or your day at school on social media. Such statements can be denigrating to the profession and may influence how others perceive your professionalism and ability to handle the demands of the job.

CHAPTER SUMMARY

Careful record keeping and documentation in special education requires an appreciation of confidentiality laws and a respect for students' rights and privacy. Along with an understanding of how to maintain and handle student records, you should know when, where, and with whom to share student information. Remember that only those with a right to know should be given educational or personal details about the student—the goal is to share what needs to be shared with appropriate team members and adults collaborating in the best interests of the child. One person should not have all the information or make all the decisions regarding the student.

The following chapter revisits the importance of the team process in making educational decisions, with an emphasis on avoiding unilateral action.

Chapter 8 Extras and Activities

How to Advise? Tackling the Tough Questions in Special Education Law

Q: I made an appointment to review my son's records, and I found several statements that were incorrect. I also found the names of at least five other students in my child's records. What should I do? Do I have the right to ask for the incorrect statements to be removed? Should I tell the other parents that their child's names are in my child's records?

A: You should put in writing what you have found in the records and you should send the information to both the records custodian and the principal and/or superintendent of the district. Always keep a copy of your request. In that letter, you should ask for a records hearing to review your concerns about the records. It is the school district's responsibility to remove other students' names in your child's records.

Interact*

- Give each participant two cards—one says "right" and the other says "wrong." Show participants the following statements, and have them raise the correct card—is it right or is it wrong?

  a. Bill, a fifth grader, has diabetes. The cafeteria supervisor has the right to know this information.

  b. A publicly posted list of student grades that identifies each student is permissible as long as it is in the classroom.

  c. A record is anything written down about a student.

  d. Any teacher in a school building has a right to view a student's online IEP.

e. It is permissible for a public school to send student records to a parochial school without the parents' permission.

- Get into a group and play a This or That activity. Put two signs up at either side of the room. Put a sign up that says "This" on one side of the room. Put a sign up that says "That" on the other side of the room. "This" denotes permanent records. "That" denotes temporary records. Read the following phrases, and have participants move to the sign indicating which type of record contains that information.

    - Birth date

    - Extracurricular activities

    - IEPs

    - Grades

    - Class standing

    - Psychological evaluations

Online Activities

- Research FERPA and find the section in the law that deals with school district responsibilities to share information when there is a public safety risk. Provide the citation.

- Research a court case that deals with FERPA and summarize the case in no more than six sentences.

Two Truths and a Lie*

Read all of these statements. Two are true, and one is a lie. Determine which one is a lie.

1. Temporary records include IEPs.

2. Confidentiality applies only to students within the school.

3. Nothing that denotes special education should be referred to in a permanent record.

*Answers for activities noted with an asterisk are provided in the Answer Key for Extras and Activities appendix.

9

Using the Team to Make Appropriate Decisions

Avoiding Unilateral Action

Teachers must make hundreds of instructional decisions every day. They are required to gather data, review the facts, consult with others when necessary, and make a decision about how to teach and manage their classroom. Decisions pertaining to the educational placement of a student with a disability rest with the IEP team, however, and not with a single individual. Changes cannot be made to the placement or program of the child without reconvening the IEP team. As stated in previous chapters, the IEP team meeting is designed for a group to review and decide on an educational plan for a student. All members of the IEP team play a critical role in the decision making for the IEP, as well as its enforcement and implementation.

There are many demands on educators in today's schools, and it is natural to want to complete tasks quickly; yet, corners cannot be cut when it pertains to IEPs. For example, a couple of teachers on an IEP team may agree that an hour increase in special education resource services per day would be the perfect solution for a student. They do not want to take the time to contact other team members and schedule another meeting, however. After all, if the two teachers meant to deliver the services have the time and are in agreement, then what harm can come from the decision? Although this example might sound like a harmless, time-saving solution, decisions like these must still be made through the IEP process.

Because the IEP is the foundational document for services for the student with a disability, the IEP team must meet when there is controversy or even a discussion about what types of services the student needs or receives. The IEP should serve as the number one guide for educators as they teach and support individual students with disabilities. A teacher may think that it is a good idea to adjust the amount of time a student receives in special education, change the services he or she receives, or even refrain from providing certain services. When questions arise, the IEP document is the legal agreement for what the student receives. If the student is not receiving services because someone changed those services unilaterally, then the parent has the right to request a due process hearing.

For example, a parent pays a visit to the special educator and asks for an evaluation for his or her child. The teacher is concerned that there is a backlog of evaluations and tells the parent that an evaluation cannot be done this year, but she can come back next year. The parent says she has signed the permission for an evaluation and wants one. The teacher apologizes but says it just cannot be done. In this instance, the teacher did not have the sole authority to determine whether to evaluate the child. When the parent makes a request for an evaluation, school personnel have an obligation to notify other members of the team and convene the evaluation team to determine whether an evaluation is needed. If an evaluation is not needed, then the team has an obligation to notify the parent in writing of the specific reasons for not conducting the evaluation. No one individual has the right to deny an evaluation unilaterally.

As a further illustration of **unilateral action** to be avoided, imagine that the occupational therapist has a large caseload and wants to move a student from 1 hour of direct service per week as stated on the IEP to a monitoring-only situation in which he or she would only check in with the classroom teacher and special education teacher once a month. Although it is the occupational therapist's place to make a recommendation like this, he or she is not permitted to make this decision without consensus of the IEP team because it would constitute a change in placement and would need to be discussed with all team members.

BASIC PRINCIPLES OF THE LAWS AND REGULATIONS REGARDING UNILATERAL ACTION

Although the term *unilateral placement* is only used in IDEA 2004 as it relates to parents making an independent decision about placement in a private educational setting and then seeking reimbursement for that private placement, the law and its regulations clearly communicate that individuals within the school system are prohibited from making unilateral placement decisions. IDEA 2004 provides for a team approach throughout the evaluation, placement, and IEP process. It is clear that the parent is an integral part of the decision-making process, and no one person makes an evaluation or placement decision.

The IEP team and other qualified professionals must review existing data, complete evaluations, and determine other information that is needed as part of any evaluation (34 C.F.R. 300.305). If the IEP team and other qualified professionals decide that no additional data are needed to determine whether the child continues to be a child with a disability and to determine the child's educational needs, then the school must notify the parents and provide the reasons (34 C.F.R. 300.305). The decision must be made by the team, not one individual.

IDEA 2004 has further guidelines regarding decisions related to the evaluation of a student. A parent has the right to request an independent educational evaluation at public expense if the parent disagrees with an evaluation conducted by the school. When a parent requests an independent educational evaluation, no individual school staff member can tell the parent "no." The IEP team should convene to review the evaluation that they have completed. Next, the school must file a due process complaint to show that the district's evaluation was appropriate or ensure that an independent educational evaluation is provided at the school's expense. If the parent requests an independent educational evaluation at public expense, then the school may ask for the parent's objections to the school's evaluation, but the school may not require the parent to provide an explanation or delay filing a due process hearing or paying for the independent evaluation (34 C.F.R. 300.502). If the parent obtains an independent educational evaluation at public expense or shares with the public agency an evaluation obtained at private expense that meets school criteria, then the school must consider the results of the evaluation when making any decisions related to providing a FAPE to the child (34 C.F.R. 300.502).

As you have read throughout this book, the collective responsibilities of the IEP team are many. Team members must include within the IEP document a statement of any individual appropriate accommodations that are necessary to measure the student's academic achievement and functional performance on state and districtwide assessments. The IEP team determines whether the student takes the alternate assessment instead of the state or districtwide assessment and why they have chosen the particular assessment (34 C.F.R. 300.320). Many issues surround assessing students with disabilities, and the IEP team as a whole must consider many factors before making a decision. The IEP team is also charged with the **consideration of special factors**—including PBIS, the child's English proficiency and language needs, the need for braille, communication needs, and assistive technology needs (20 U.S.C 1414 and 34 C.F.R. 300.324).

All IEP team members should also be involved in making any changes to the IEP. A parent of a child with a disability and the local educational agency can agree not to convene an IEP meeting for making changes. Changes may be made either by the entire IEP team at an IEP team meeting or by amending the IEP rather than redrafting the entire document. If changes are made to the child's IEP, then the school must ensure that every member of the child's IEP team, including the parent, is informed of those changes (34 C.F.R. 300.324; 20 U.S.C. Section 1414). The team can "develop a written document to amend or modify the child's current IEP" (20 U.S.C. Section 1414).

IDEA 2004 also has clear guidelines for decisions regarding student placement. School personnel may remove a child with a disability who violates a code of student conduct from his or her current placement to an appropriate interim alternative educational placement, another setting, or suspension for not more than 10 consecutive school days. After a child with a disability has been removed from his or her current placement for 10 school days in the same school year, the school must provide services during any subsequent days of removal (34 C.F.R. 300.530). School personnel should be careful not to suspend students unilaterally because if the suspension of less than 10 days is made without good reason, then the staff member who suspended the student can be questioned. An organized, outlined process for giving suspensions should be implemented. If staff members are unilaterally suspending students and have not communicated with the parent and other school personnel, then they may have exceeded the 10 days if there is not a coordinated plan for giving and tracking suspensions.

This chapter's mnemonic provides tips for making team decisions.

The following How Would You Rule? exercise presents a case in which a school district decided to withdraw services from a student who was exhibiting

---

Just 3 X 5 It: A Mnemonic to Help You Remember

We must CARE enough about the needs of the student to make decisions through the individualized education program (IEP) team process. Avoid acting unilaterally by exercising CARE.

C—Consult with others and convene the IEP team when a decision will affect the student's placement.

A—Ask the right questions.

R—Review the records before participating in the IEP.

E—Evaluate all options. Remember that the responsibility of the IEP team is to develop possible options for the student and then evaluate each option to come up with the most appropriate decision to meet the student's needs.

---

aggressive and potentially unsafe behavior. Do you think that the school district was justified in its decision?

How Would You Rule?

A student with a psychiatric disorder transferred to a new school district in Wisconsin in 2012. The IEP from the previous district had not provided information about the student's academic functioning. In the new school, the student was only provided one-to-one instruction by a teacher for 2 hours per week after regular school hours, and the instruction focused on behavior. A new IEP meeting was convened to determine this specific placement.

The student became physically aggressive with the teacher during the second week of the student's instruction. The teacher was afraid of the student. As a result, the district believed that it did not have a duty to educate the student until the student was prepared for school. Therefore, the district immediately decided to no longer provide services.

Your ruling:

_____

_____

_____

_____

The court's ruling:

The U.S. District Court ruled in *Vincent ex rel. B.V. v. Kenosha Unified Sch. Dist.* (2012) that it was acceptable to develop the IEP that only focused on behavior, but it ruled that it was unacceptable to discontinue the student's services for 2 hours daily based on the safety concerns of one teacher. The decision should have been made by the entire IEP team.

CASE STUDY COMPARISON

The everyday demands of the school day and expectations of the job make it tempting for individuals to make unilateral decisions rather than consulting other members of the educational team. An administrator in the first example is under pressure and makes an inappropriate decision for students without following the IEP and going through the proper channels. A teacher in the exemplary approach makes the right choice to stick by the student and the IEP. Both stories offer important lessons about utilizing the team process.

A Case of Missteps and Mistakes

A great deal of stress is felt at Merrygrove School about the administration of the state assessment. Mr. Roberts has come to Merrygrove as a new principal and did not have the advantage of participating in the previous year's IEPs for the students in Mrs. Holden's instructional cross-categorical special education classroom. There are 10 students in the classroom—two students will participate in an alternate assessment, and the other students will take the statewide assessment with the specific accommodations listed in their IEPs. Mr. Roberts does not believe that the students who will take the statewide assessment should really take the test. He is concerned that these students will lower the scores of the school and district. He confers with the teacher, and she relays to him what the students' IEPs say. Still, Mr. Roberts is determined that the students will not participate in the assessment. He tells Mrs. Holden that if she wants to give the alternate assessment to the two students, then that is fine with him, but the others will not take the regular assessment. He also says that he is going to recommend that all of the students take the alternate assessment when the new IEPs are due. The teacher tries to explain that only 1% of the student population, those with the most significant intellectual disabilities, can take the alternate assessment.

Mr. Roberts lets the teacher know that, as the administrator, he makes the final decision on who takes the assessment. Mr. Roberts sends a note home to the parents of the children in Mrs. Holden's instructional class (except the two taking the alternate assessment), telling them that their children should not plan to attend school on the days of the state assessment. He has decided the students should not take the test. He explains to the parents that he is looking out for the best interest of the students and believes they should just stay home.

What errors were made in this example? Consider the following missteps and mistakes:

- Mr. Roberts acted unilaterally and unethically. He had the knowledge that the students in Mrs. Holden's class were to take the state assessment with specific accommodations. He was worried that the scores of the students would affect his school's status, and he did not want to lower his school's scores. He ignored the IEPs of the students and acted on his own.

How should Mr. Roberts have proceeded in this example? What could Mrs. Holden have done?

- Mr. Roberts should have reviewed the IEPs of the students and followed the IEPs' instruction to provide the state assessment with the appropriate accommodations. If he did not agree that the assessment with accommodations was appropriate for the eight students, then he should have reconvened the IEP team to determine the assessment arrangements. He alone would not make that decision—it would be through team consensus.

- Mrs. Holden could have asked for a new IEP meeting to discuss the accommodations and could have provided the necessary documentation that showed what the students needed for an appropriate assessment.

The Exemplary Approach

Mr. Cory has been a special education teacher for 5 years. He co-teaches one part of the day and provides resource special education services for the rest of the day. His caseload is larger this year than in past years, and he finds himself very busy. One of his co-teachers, a fifth-grade teacher, wants him to work longer in her classroom during the day. Mr. Cory reviews each of his students' IEPs to see whether he is providing exactly what those IEPs say. He is providing the number of minutes that is outlined on each student's IEP. He explains this to the fifth-grade teacher. The fifth-grade teacher suggests that he reduce the time for Andre, one of his resource students, and that would give him more time to be in her classroom. Mr. Cory explains that he is unable to do that without a new IEP. The fifth-grade teacher is upset and goes to the principal. The principal then approaches Mr. Cory and asks him why he cannot spend more time in the fifth-grade classroom, requesting that Mr. Cory reduce the amount of time that Andre is seen. Mr. Cory is upset that the fifth-grade teacher went around him and went to the principal, but he knows the importance of remaining professional and following the IEP. He explains to the principal that he believes the amount of time on Andre's IEP is exactly what Andre needs, but a new IEP meeting can be scheduled. The principal decides that this will not be necessary and Mr. Cory should continue to provide the services that Andre needs. Mr. Cory is worried about the relationship that he has with the fifth-grade teacher. He wants to assist her, but knows it is not possible. He decides to meet with her and explain how he must follow the IEP. He asks her how she needs additional assistance and whether there is any other way he can help. She explains that she is having some difficulty making all the accommodations her students need. Mr. Cory agrees to work with her to see if there are other ways he can assist her that would not require him to be in her classroom.

SOLUTIONS TO COMMON MISTAKES

The following mistakes are common errors seen in educational decision making. Solutions focus on careful collaboration and attention to the law.

Mistake: Failure to review information on the student's IEP before making any decision

Solution: Competent educators learn to make informed decisions. They do not make snap decisions and realize the ramifications later, but they gather information before making a decision for any student. As part of the information-gathering process for students with disabilities, educators must review the most recent IEP and interview any IEP implementers to make sure that any change in supports or instruction will not affect the IEP. If so, then the proposed change should be a collective decision made by the IEP team.

Mistake: Failure to schedule a new IEP meeting when a change in the student's IEP might be made or a significant change in the child's progress or specific needs is occurring

Solution: The special educator must monitor the special education programming that is outlined in the student's IEP. Special educators will ask me questions such as the following: "Can I remove the student from his social work services? He does not seem to want to go." "Can I change the statewide assessment for this student?" "Can I decrease the time that the student receives speech-language services?" My response to these questions is, "What does the IEP say?"

The IEP is the binding document that governs the placement of the student. The decisions outlined within the IEP reflect team consensus and should govern placement and related services until a new IEP meeting is convened or the IEP is properly amended. The special educator should request a new IEP meeting when he or she believes that a change is needed in placement and/or related services provided to the student. There are also provisions for providing an addendum to the IEP, which are covered in this book.

Multiple factors may cause a change in the student's needs and necessitate revising the IEP. For instance, you may have students within your special education programs that have multiple medical needs, and their medications are periodically changed. Changes in medication may cause profound positive or negative changes in a student's behavior. The IEP may have been conducted when the child's behavior was under control and there was no need to develop a BIP. Then, the medication is adjusted or new medications are introduced, causing behavioral side effects. Or, the student or parent discontinues the medication, and the child begins to have multiple behavior problems. A BIP is now needed because the behavior is definitely interfering with educational performance. The IEP meeting must be reconvened to develop a BIP based on an FBA.

Mistake: Disregard for teacher or parent request for an evaluation or a new IEP meeting

Solution: Whenever a parent or teacher requests an evaluation, it is a good idea to ask that the individual make the request in writing (although the parent can verbally request an evaluation, and that verbal request should not be ignored). The educators must convene the IEP team, including evaluators and the parent, so the team can determine whether an evaluation is needed. The decision of the team must then be provided in writing to the parent.

Mistake: Disregard for parent request for an independent evaluation at public expense

Solution: If the parent is dissatisfied with the evaluation conducted by the school district, then the parent does have the right to request an independent evaluation at the school district's expense. School personnel must then act promptly, collectively deciding to either file a due process hearing to show that the evaluation from the school district was appropriate or choosing to have the school district pay for the evaluation.

A preventive strategy should be used prior to a request for an independent evaluation. When the special educator learns that the parent is dissatisfied with an evaluation, he or she should find out what the dissatisfaction is about and arrange a meeting with the parent and the evaluator to answer any questions. School personnel may also want to check to see if the school district has another member of the evaluation team employed by the district who could conduct an additional evaluation.

Mistake: Disregard for an independent evaluation that the parent provides to the school system. This is a common problem that I see within schools. The parent has an outside, independent evaluation conducted by a physician, clinical psychologist, psychiatrist, or some other evaluator. The parent provides the evaluation to school personnel, who put it in the student's temporary record or give it to the special education teacher. Nothing else is done with the evaluation.

In another scenario, the parent tells the special educator that he or she has had an independent evaluation conducted, or the teacher tells the administrator that he or she has heard that the parent took the child to a psychiatrist and the psychiatrist is upset with the programming for the student.

Solution: Any independent evaluation that is conducted and received by the school district must be recognized by the school district. The IEP team does not have to accept the results of the evaluation, but must acknowledge the evaluation and convene for the purpose of reviewing the results. School personnel who receive a copy of an evaluation report must provide notice of an IEP meeting, notify participants that the purpose is to review the results of an independent evaluation, and convene the IEP team.

In the scenario in which school personnel are told that the parent has an independent evaluation, but the school district has not received the evaluation, school personnel should ask for a copy of the evaluation, or the administrator should request it. Some school personnel contend that if the parents do not give them a copy, then it is of no concern to them. The district may be asked in a hearing why they did not make a request for a copy if school personnel knew that there was an independent evaluation.

School personnel cannot request a copy directly from the source of the evaluation unless the parent has signed a written release for the information. If the parent has not signed a release, then the only avenue to get the evaluation is through the parent. Once again, school personnel may not act unilaterally concerning evaluations.

CHAPTER SUMMARY

Decision making for the student should be an informed process involving the family and all educational team members. School personnel should be collaborative, proactive, and professional when adhering to special education law and serving their students, essential qualities repeatedly stressed throughout this book. The final chapter discusses your role and image as an educator. In a job that can be equally stressful and rewarding, our outlook and behaviors can make a substantial difference in the educational field, in the lives of our students, and in our personal and professional happiness.

Chapter 9 Extras and Activities

How to Advise? Tackling the Tough Questions in Special Education Law

Q: I have a son who is 10 years old and is in a program for students identified with emotional and behavior disorders. He was recently suspended from school for 12 days for what the principal described as dangerous behavior. My son poked a pencil at another student. I asked the principal whether the jab broke the other child's skin. The principal said that it did not, but that he was able to suspend for 12 days because he has that prerogative. Is this correct, and, if so, where does it say that in the law?

A: The principal cannot unilaterally suspend the student for 12 days. He is able to make the decision to suspend for 10 days and must convene the multidisciplinary team to determine whether the student's behavior was related to his disability. IDEA 2004 allows for up to 10 days of suspension but not more without convening the IEP team to determine the relationship between the behavior and the disability.

Interact*

- Give each participant two cards—one that says "yes" and one that says "no." Ask whether unilateral action is allowed for the following decisions. Participants raise their card with the appropriate answer.

  a. The principal decides what testing accommodations can be given.

  b. The teacher changes the amount of time a student sees the SLP.

  c. The teacher sends a student home for the rest of the day because of the student's behavior.

  d. The teacher changes the order of when reading and math take place on one day.

  e. The principal determines that an independent evaluation that a parent had done is not important.

- Discuss why it is important to make decisions that pertain to the IEP needs of the student as part of an IEP team meeting. Ask your colleagues or fellow preservice teachers whether they have ever witnessed an individual making a unilateral decision without the IEP team involvement. Tell them not to give anyone's name.

- As part of an in-service activity, mingle with other colleagues and ask them whether they have ever taken a unilateral action that they should not have taken. Or, do an informal poll on the number of colleagues who say they have versus those who say they have not.

Online Activities

- Find a court case in which an individual within the school made a unilateral decision about a student's placement. Cite the case, specify who won the case, and explain what could have been done differently.

Two Truths and a Lie*

Read all of these statements. Two are true, and one is a lie. Determine which one is a lie.

1. School personnel may unilaterally suspend a student for not more than 10 school days.

2. School district personnel who are requesting an IEP meeting that includes developing a transition plan do not have to invite a representative of an agency that provides postschool services if they do not believe the agency representative will attend anyway.

3. The school principal should invite a classroom teacher to the IEP meeting even though the student is placed in a specialized school.

*Answers for activities noted with an asterisk are provided in the Answer Key for Extras and Activities appendix.

10

Presenting a Positive Image

Monitoring Yourself Inside and Outside School

Albert Einstein said, "Example isn't another way to teach; it is the only way to teach." We are representatives and ambassadors of our profession by what we say and do. It is easy for us to grow frustrated and become negative about our work when education and special education are continually in the news and those outside the field want to reform policy and practice. People outside the field of education do not always understand the job we do or the needs of our students. People may make assumptions and prejudicial statements about students with disabilities, so we must work constantly to do our jobs, try to break those barriers of misunderstanding, and educate those in the community and in decision-making positions. Even when we are discouraged, we must continually portray a positive image of what we do as ambassadors of our profession and students with special needs. We can only project that image by monitoring our own behavior inside and outside of school.

People may assume that we do not like our profession when they hear us complaining about everything we have to do and that we never get any support. Although it is human to vent our frustrations, continual complaining is not productive. Rather, we must educate those around us so we can work together to provide better supports and services for students with disabilities and special needs. Building strong, collaborative teams sets a good example for colleagues and promotes future teamwork.

It is also important to uphold the ethics of our profession, and we must put that foremost in our mind while on the job. Regularly engaging with local and national professional associations, maintaining credentials, and participating in professional development can help keep the job fresh and the work inspiring. You have learned throughout this book about a number of ethical violations that can and do occur in our school systems. As this chapter is being written, there have been two major instances in the news. One dealt with a special education teacher who threatened to blow up a school in a moment of anger. In another instance, an educator was accused of inappropriate sexual activity. Although these are extreme cases, they remind us that the behavior of such individuals can jeopardize the trust and confidence that people have in educators and in schools being safe places for students.

Those of us who are educators are public servants and must conduct ourselves in a professional manner. How we act, what we say, and what type of image we project is important. Some educators think they are off the clock when they are not at school. That is not to say that teachers cannot enjoy themselves outside of school; of course there will be parties and evenings out. Your personal life is still yours. It is important to remember, however, that you are setting an example in and out of school, and your private life is not always so private, particularly when you consider how much people share via social media such as Facebook, Twitter, and Instagram.

It is appropriate to end this book with this chapter because you are now knowledgeable about the law and understand its intricacies. You have learned how important it is to follow the law because you are affecting a child and his or her family's life in your everyday work. Your role as a professional educator is held to high standards and expectations.

BASIC PRINCIPLES OF THE LAWS AND REGULATIONS REGARDING OUR SPEECH AND BEHAVIOR AS EDUCATORS

Some educators may believe that they are protected by the Constitution's First Amendment, which provides freedom of speech, when it comes to their speech and behavior outside of school. This is not always correct, however. Teachers might not be protected when their actions result in a damaged relationship with students and parents or when their speech is disruptive to school activities. I often hear educators (and plenty of other people) say that they have the right to post anything they want on Facebook or other social media outlets and there should be no ramifications. Yet, administrators and supervisors do a thorough Internet search, including Facebook and other social media sites, as a part of the hiring process. Administrators can also check an employed teacher's Facebook page, and if material being posted is inappropriate, then the teacher can jeopardize his or her ability to achieve tenure. Although teachers are working for tenure, many might not have their contract renewed, and they may not be provided with a reason (Simpson, 2010).

Although they are provided some protections with regard to out-of-school conduct, educators are held to a higher standard of conduct than the general public because they are considered role models for students (Eckes, 2013). The following two court cases help clarify the protections afforded and not afforded to educators.

A high school science teacher was terminated from his position by the school board for writing a letter to the editor of a local newspaper that criticized the board of education for utilizing school funds for academics and athletics (*Pickering v. Board of Education*, 1968). The teacher then sued the district because he felt it denied his right to free speech. With a vote of 8-1, the U.S. Supreme Court held that school employees are entitled to some First Amendment protections, and school officials do violate the First Amendment when they terminate an employee for speaking out as citizens in matters of public concern. The science teacher was speaking as a citizen.

In another case, Jeffrey Spanierman, a nontenured English teacher in Connecticut, opened a MySpace account and created several profiles, one of which was named Mr. Spiderman (*Spanierman v. Hughes,* 2008). The account was used to communicate with students about homework and to have related discussions. There were complaints that some of the posts were inappropriate and even had pictures of naked men. He stopped using Mr. Spiderman and initiated another profile. Complaints continued to be made by students to the guidance counselor, who reported these concerns to her boss, who then made a report to the principal. Following more investigation, Jeffrey Spanierman received a written notice that his contract would not be renewed. He then filed suit, saying that his 14th Amendment rights of due process and equal protection were violated, as was his First Amendment right to freedom of expression and association. The court ruled that the First Amendment did not provide protection because almost none of the contents of his profile page dealt with matters of public concern (Zirkel, 2008). The court also believed that his speech was disrupting school activities.

Many courts have adopted a **nexus theory** that teachers' off-duty conduct might result in a negative impact on their teaching effectiveness (Eckes, 2013). The courts will look at whether the actions of the teacher resulted in damaged relationships with students and parents.

This book's final mnemonic is a call for professionalism in our role as educators, with strategies for getting the most out of the teaching profession, refining our image, and enacting positive change.

Just 3 X 5 It: A Mnemonic to Help You Remember

We are PROFESSIONAL.

P—Pride in our profession: We work in an extremely important profession in which we can and do make a positive difference in the lives of our students and their families.

R—Respect: It is critical that we treat students, families, and our colleagues with respect.

O—Opportunity: We are given the opportunity every day to work with students, and we should always view our profession as a wonderful opportunity for personal growth and positive change.

F—Firm: We must stand firm in our convictions to do the right thing, even when we may be pressured to act otherwise.

E—Ethical: We must continually monitor our own behavior to ensure that we are acting in an ethical manner.

S—Support: Our profession calls for us to support our colleagues, the children we serve, and the families with whom we partner.

(continued)

(continued)

> **S**—Social media: Any public posting using social media should be utilized to build and not tear down our profession.
>
> **I**—Interest: We must ask ourselves first and foremost, "Is what we are doing in the best interest of our students?"
>
> **O**—Observe: Before making a judgment about a situation, we should observe and learn as much as possible about the situation and not pass judgment until we have all the facts.
>
> **N**—No harm: Our motto should always be "first, do no harm."
>
> **A**—Actions: Our actions speak louder than words, and every action we take should be professional and should focus on the fact that we are role models for our students and their families.
>
> **L**—Lifelong learners: Each day we are reminded that we never have all the answers and must continue to grow professionally and personally.

This chapter's How Would You Rule? exercise invites you to analyze a teacher's out-of-the-classroom behavior on the Internet. How do you think this situation should have been handled by the district?

How Would You Rule?

A teacher was a mentor for other teachers with less experience. This teacher had a publicly available blog that included personal and negative comments about her employers, fellow teachers, and union representatives. This teacher did not refer to the individuals by name, but some said they were easy to identify because of the descriptions of their positions. There were several complaints, including one from an individual to whom the teacher was assigned as an instructional coach. The district transferred this teacher on the grounds that her blog undermined her ability to enter into a trusting relationship with colleagues and fulfill her role as an instructional coach. Should the teacher have been transferred?

Your ruling:

_____
_____
_____
_____

The court's ruling:

It was determined in *Tara L. Richerson v. Jeanne Beckon* (2009) that Richerson's speech had a significantly detrimental effect because several individuals refused to work with her. Not many teachers would believe that they could enter into a confidential and trusting relationship with her. The district could make a reasonable prediction that disruption would occur. It was determined that a great deal of deference is given to the employer's judgment when close working relationships are essential to fulfilling public responsibilities. Therefore, Richerson could be transferred.

CASE STUDY COMPARISON

The first study displays the downside of allowing frustrations and negativity to dominate your day-to-day work and behavior outside of the classroom. A teacher in the exemplary approach example embraces a positive outlook, even in the face of stress, setting a strong example for her students and colleagues.

A Case of Missteps and Mistakes

George is worn out from all the paperwork he has to do. He is working hard and does not believe he is appreciated. He has gotten bogged down with the number of IEPs that he is expected to complete. George loves to utilize social media, and at the end of a long day, he likes to share his day on Facebook. His most recent post says, "I am so tired of all these IEPs I have to do. I sure wish I could just teach and not have to do all these meetings in which half of the parents do not even show up. What is the point, anyway?"

What errors do you see in this example? Consider the list of missteps and mistakes:

- What kind of message is George sending to his Facebook friends? He is devaluing the importance of the individualized education programs for each of his students. The IEP determines the future of a child's education and is very important to the child's success or lack thereof at school. George is actually making a public statement that he wishes IEPs would be eliminated and he could just teach. However, it is the IEP document that charts the course for his teaching.

- George is downgrading the profession and speaking against individualization. A legislator may read this and think that special education programs should be eliminated. Those who advocate for high-quality special education programs read the message and view it as offensive to those who are trying to promote excellence in special education programs.

- George is also making a negative statement about the parents of his students. He is not explaining why the parents might not be attending the IEP meeting. Perhaps they do not feel welcome by him. What has he done to encourage their participation? How does he make parents feel when they do attend the IEP meeting? Perhaps the parents have other obligations that prevented them from attending. A member of the community might read this message and become upset by the derogatory statements toward parents.

How can George better monitor his behavior and project a more positive image?

- Before George sends any type of message, he should review it and closely investigate how it may be interpreted by individuals reading it.

- George should vow that he will not make statements that may be offensive to the parents of his students. If he wants to work collaboratively with parents, then he must continue to make an effort and should communicate respect.

The Exemplary Approach

Janette takes her responsibility as a special educator seriously. She has been in the profession for 10 years and has learned that it is important to project a positive image of her work and convey a professional attitude every day. She is a user of social media and makes a point to never put any negative posts about her work. Her posts focus on positive comments about what is happening in her life and her professional world. When she hears other individuals complaining about their jobs, she does not buy in and instead changes the focus of the conversation to something positive. She makes it a point to dress up for school every day. Although there are days when she could wear jeans, she will not do that because she believes that she owes her students her best dress.

Before passing judgments on others, she listens to all sides of the story and does not make negative statements about others. She is participating in an IEP meeting for one of her students that she has about 50% of the time. Her student is in general education classes the other part of the day. The student is having some behavioral concerns, and two of the teachers who see the student begin making negative and subjective statements about the child. Janette refocuses the discussion and asks the teachers some questions about available data on the student's behavior. She then discusses the strengths that she sees within the student and asks the teachers whether they are seeing particular strengths. The parent becomes upset with the other teachers because of their negativity and starts yelling at them out of frustration. Janette continues to speak in a calm tone of voice and asks the parent how she can help with the student.

SOLUTIONS TO COMMON MISTAKES

The following solutions can help us improve our professional image and avoid negativity in our school and in the field at large.

Mistake: Posting negative comments about your work, photographs of yourself in revealing clothing, or photographs of yourself with alcoholic drinks in hand on Facebook or other social media

Solution: Adopt this adage: "Never post anything on Facebook that you do not want the world to see." We may want to show that we are having a good time in a setting, but be careful when posting a photograph if it is not an image that you would want to project to the public.

Mistake: Sending an angry or negative e-mail to a parent or colleague

Solution: Be careful about what you put in an e-mail to anyone. Avoid sending an e-mail when you are upset, and wait until you have calmed down. Even then, reread the e-mail before sending it. Remember that an e-mail is in cyberspace permanently.

Mistake: Sending an e-mail to several people when it is meant for one person

Solution: When you want to send a response to one individual, be careful that you do not hit the reply all button by accident. I can remember receiving an e-mail from someone commenting that he or she thought I was wrong on an issue. The person meant to send the e-mail to one person and had hit the reply all button by mistake, so I received the e-mail.

Mistake: Making a negative statement about an individual or individuals via e-mail and sending it to a particular person

Solution: Avoid doing this because you never know when the individual who you sent the e-mail to may decide to forward it to someone else.

CHAPTER SUMMARY

We must carefully examine our attitudes, outlooks, and activities and see how they are affecting our professional image as well as our colleagues, students, and their families. By law, we can be held accountable for our actions, even those outside of school, if they have an adverse effect on the children and families that we are serving. Hopefully, you come away from this final chapter with a newfound desire to be the best educator possible and with strategies for getting the most out of your career. There is no doubt that the field of special education is not only full of exacting challenges but also unlimited opportunity. Together, we can help children thrive and succeed at life, regardless of their challenge or disability.

Chapter 10 Extras and Activities

How to Advise? Tackling the Tough Questions in Special Education Law

Q: There is currently a group of parents who are meeting to make plans to oppose the closing of a school. There has been a lot of press coverage about this, and the evening meeting is open to the public. I want to attend; however, the principal has announced that no teacher is allowed to go to the meeting. Does the principal have the right to tell me I cannot attend an evening meeting? I am a new teacher, so I do not want to lose my job, but I also do not agree with the school closing. What should I do?

A: As a new teacher, you are vulnerable in the school district. The principal may not have had the right to tell you that you could not attend the meeting, which is a public meeting and is not taking place during work hours. The principal, however, will probably be upset with you because you chose to defy his order (right or wrong) and could use that information as a way to not re-employ you.

Interact

- Get into a small group of colleagues or fellow preservice teachers to discuss the following situations and whether the educators are acting as positive role models for students and their families.

- Mr. Sunderson believes that he should be able to wear what he wants to school, even though the school has a dress code. He does not believe the dress code should apply to teachers.

- Mrs. Benton has a Facebook account under a disguised name, and she believes that she should be able to post what she wants on her page because she is not identifying herself with her real name.

- Mrs. Danielson and Mrs. Garcia have playground duty together, and they love to talk about the superintendent negatively and complain about his actions.

- Discuss and reflect on the components of an effective school district policy on appropriate behavior outside school with colleagues or fellow preservice teachers.

- Interview five colleagues or fellow students and ask them whether they are familiar with the code of ethics for their profession.

Online Activities

- Research a story featured in your own state that involved a teacher being released for inappropriate conduct. Critique the story and provide your opinion on what the teacher could have done to prevent him- or herself from getting into that situation.

- Peruse some Facebook posts over a period of 1 week and determine how many of those statements involved negative comments about the individual's role as an educator.

- Review the Council for Exceptional Children's Code of Ethics (2015) and provide a summary of it.

Two Truths and a Lie*

Read all of these statements. Two are true, and one is a lie. Determine which one is a lie.

1. Off-duty conduct can be considered when determining whether an individual should be reemployed.

2. What a school district employee posts on Facebook is no business of the school district.

3. Educators are not always protected by the Constitution's First Amendment of freedom of speech.

*Answers for activities noted with an asterisk are provided in the Answer Key for Extras and Activities appendix.

Conclusion

You have taken the first step in being well informed about the rights of students with disabilities and your responsibility in implementing the laws that have been developed. This book has been designed to give you an overview of the legal issues of working with students with special needs. It is hoped that you will utilize this guide frequently as you have questions about the laws and regulations. If you want to look up the specific references in the law or regulations themselves, those references are provided to you throughout this book.

Knowledge, however, is not enough. Knowledge has to translate into action. You now have gained knowledge so you can act responsibly in your everyday profession. You are acting on behalf of students and their families to ensure that they are afforded the right to a free and appropriate public education. You are in a noble profession, and your knowledge and action must always reflect the importance of what you are doing.

Your responsibility is great. Gain knowledge. Translate that knowledge into your practice. All students count on you.

References

CHAPTER 1

20 U.S.C. Section 1401.

20 U.S.C. Section 1414.

34 U.S.C. Section 1412(c)(25).

Americans with Disabilities Amendments Act (ADA) of 2008, PL 110-325, 42 U.S.C. §§ 12101 *et seq.*

Bd. Ed. Hendrick Hudson Sch. Dist. v. Amy Rowley, 458 U.S. 176 (1982).

Burlington Sch. Comm. v. Mass. Dept. Ed., 471 U.S. 359 (1985).

Cedar Rapids Community School Dist. v. Garret F., 526 U.S. 66 (1999).

Clyde K. and Sheila K. individually and as guardians for Ryan K. v. Puyallup School District, 21 IDELR 664 (September 13, 1994).

Doug C. v. State of Hawaii Department of Education, 61 IDELR 91 (9th Circuit, 2013).

Education for All Handicapped Children Act of 1975, PL 94-142, 20 U.S.C. §§ 1400 *et seq.*

Florence County School District Four v. Shannon Carter, 510 U.S. 7 (1993).

Forest Grove School District v. T.A., 129 S. Ct. 2484 (2009).

Honig v. Doe, 484 U.S. 305 (1988).

Individuals with Disabilities Education Act Regulations, 34 C.F.R. 300.17.

Individuals with Disabilities Education Act Regulations, 34 C.F.R. 300.39.

Individuals with Disabilities Education Act Regulations, 34 C.F.R. 300.114.

Individuals with Disabilities Education Act Regulations, 34 C.F.R. 300.300.

Individuals with Disabilities Education Act Regulations, 34 C.F.R. 300.304.

Individuals with Disabilities Education Act Regulations, 34 C.F.R. 300.320.

Individuals with Disabilities Education Improvement Act (IDEA) of 2004, PL 108-446, 20 U.S.C. §§ 1400 *et seq.*

Irving Indep. Sch. Dist. v. Amber Tatro, 468 U.S. 883 (1984).

Johns, B. (2011). *401 practical adaptations for every classroom.* Thousand Oaks, CA: Corwin.

Lerner, J., & Johns, B. (2015). *Learning disabilities and related disabilities: Strategies for success (13th ed.).* Stamford, CT: Cengage.

Musgrove, M. (2011). *A response to intervention (RTI) process cannot be used to delay-deny an evaluation for eligibility under the Individuals with Disabilities Education Act (IDEA).* Washington, D.C.: United States Department of Education, Office of Special Education and Rehabilitative Services.

Rehabilitation Act of 1973, PL 93-112, 29 U.S.C. §§ 701 *et seq.*

Sacramento City Unified School District Board of Education v. Rachel H., 20 IDELR 182 (1994).

Slater, A. (2014). *The special education 2014 desk book.* Palm Beach Gardens, FL: LRP Publications.

United States Government Accountability Office. (Published August 25, 2014 and publicly released September 24, 2014). *Improved Performance Measures Could Enhance Oversight of Dispute Resolution.* Retrieved from gao.gov/products/GAO-14-390

Zobrest v. Catalina Foothills School Dist., 509 U.S. 1 (1993).

CHAPTER 2

Evans, R. (2004). Talking with parents today. *Independent School, 63*(3), 1–6.

Individuals with Disabilities Education Act Regulations, 34 C.F.R. 300.9.

Individuals with Disabilities Education Act Regulations, 34 C.F.R. 300.30.

Individuals with Disabilities Education Act Regulations, 34 C.F.R. 300.34.

Individuals with Disabilities Education Act Regulations, 34 C.F.R. 300.300.

Individuals with Disabilities Education Act Regulations, 34 C.F.R. 300.322.

Individuals with Disabilities Education Act Regulations, 34 C.F.R. 300.324.

Individuals with Disabilities Education Act Regulations, 34 C.F.R. 300.504.

Individuals with Disabilities Education Improvement Act (IDEA) of 2004, PL 108-446, 20 U.S.C. §§ 1400 *et seq.*

Jones, L., Hastings, R., Totsika, V., Keane, L., & Rhule, N. (2014). Child behavior problems and parental well-being in families of children with autism: The mediating role of mindfulness and acceptance. *American Journal of Intellectual and Developmental Disabilities, 119*(2), 171–185.

Joshi, A., Eberly, J., & Konzal, J. (2005). Dialogue across cultures: Teachers' perceptions about communication with diverse families. *Multicultural Education, 13,* 11–15.

Martin, J., Van Dycke, J., Greene, B., Gardner, J., Christensen, W., Woods, L. (2006). Direct observation of teacher-directed IEP meetings: Establishing the need for student IEP meeting instruction. *Exceptional Children, 72,* 187–200.

McNaughton, D., & Vostal, B. (2010). Using active listening to improve collaboration with parents: The LAFF don't Cry strategy. *Intervention in School and Clinic, 45*(4), 251–256.

Nalu Y. by Patty and Lee Y. v. Department of Educ., State of Hawaii (2012). Retrieved from https://www.gpo.gov/fdsys/pkg/USCOURTS-hid-1_11-cv-00067/pdf/USCOURTS-hid-1_11-cv-00067-0.pdf

CHAPTER 3

20 U.S.C. 1412.

20 U.S.C. 1414.

Giangreco, M., Suter, J., & Hurley, S. (2011). Revisiting personnel utilizing in inclusion-oriented schools. *Journal of Special Education, 47*(2), 121–132.

Individuals with Disabilities Education Act Regulations, 34 C.F.R. 300.306.

Individuals with Disabilities Education Act Regulations, 34 C.F.R. 300.321.

Individuals with Disabilities Education Improvement Act (IDEA) of 2004, PL 108-446, 20 U.S.C. §§ 1400 *et seq.*

Johns, B. (2014). *Getting behavioral interventions right: Proper uses to avoid common abuses.* Palm Beach Gardens, FL: LRP Publications.

Richmond, M. (2014, August). *The hidden half: School employees who don't teach.* Washington, DC: Thomas Fordham Institute.

Slater, A. (2014). *The special education 2014 desk book.* Palm Beach Gardens, FL: LRP publications.

V.M. v. North Colonie Central School District, 61 IDELR 134 (N.D.N.Y. 2013).

CHAPTER 4

20 U.S.C. 1401.

20 U.S.C. 1414.

20 U.S.C. 1436.

Bateman, B., & Herr, C. (2006). *Writing measurable IEP goals and objectives.* Verona, WI: Attainment Company.

Center for Parent Information and Resources. (2010). *Program modifications for school personnel.* Retrieved from http://www.parentcenterhub.org/repository/modifications-personnel

Education for All Handicapped Children Act of 1975, PL 94-142, 20 U.S.C. §§ 1400 *et seq.*

Individuals with Disabilities Education Act Regulations, 34 C.F.R. 300.8.

Individuals with Disabilities Education Act Regulations, 34 C.F.R. 300.30.

Individuals with Disabilities Education Act Regulations, 34 C.F.R. 300.39.

Individuals with Disabilities Education Act Regulations, 34 C.F.R. 300.42.

Individuals with Disabilities Education Act Regulations, 34 C.F.R. 300.43.

Individuals with Disabilities Education Act Regulations, 34 C.F.R. 300.106.

Individuals with Disabilities Education Act Regulations, 34 C.F.R. 300.107.

Individuals with Disabilities Education Act Regulations, 34 C.F.R. 300.108.

Individuals with Disabilities Education Act Regulations, 34 C.F.R. 300.114.

Individuals with Disabilities Education Act Regulations, 34 C.F.R. 300.115.

Individuals with Disabilities Education Act Regulations, 34 C.F.R. 300.132.
Individuals with Disabilities Education Act Regulations, 34 C.F.R. 300.133.
Individuals with Disabilities Education Act Regulations, 34 C.F.R. 300.300.
Individuals with Disabilities Education Act Regulations, 34 C.F.R. 300.320.
Individuals with Disabilities Education Act Regulations, 34 C.F.R. 300.321.
Individuals with Disabilities Education Act Regulations, 34 C.F.R. 300.322.
Individuals with Disabilities Education Act Regulations, 34 C.F.R. 300.323.
Individuals with Disabilities Education Act Regulations, 34 C.F.R. 300.324.
Individuals with Disabilities Education Act Regulations, 34 C.F.R. 300.328.
Individuals with Disabilities Education Improvement Act (IDEA) of 2004, PL 108-446, 20 U.S.C. §§ 1400 *et seq.*
Jefferson County Board of Education v. Lolita S. (2014). Retrieved from: http://law.justia.com/cases/federal/appellate-courts/ca11/13-15170/13-15170-2014-09-11.html
Pennsylvania State Education Association. (2015). *Teaching students with disabilities: LRE, educational placement and the Gaskin Settlement.* Retrieved from https://www.psea.org/uploadedFiles/TeachingandLearning/LRE%20and%20Gaskin.pdf
Tierney, J. (2011, August 17). Do you suffer from decision fatigue? *The New York Times.* Retrieved from http://www.nytimes.com/2011/08/21/magazine/do-you-suffer-from-decision-fatigue.html. In print in *New York Times,* Sunday magazine, To Choose is to Lose, print on August 21, 2011, page mm33.
Winterman, K.G., & Rosas, C.E. (2014). *The IEP checklist: Your guide to creating meaningful and compliant IEPs.* Baltimore, MD: Paul H. Brookes Publishing Co.

CHAPTER 5

DeMitchell, T. (2007). *Negligence: What principals need to know about avoiding liability.* Lanham, MD: Rowman and Littlefield Education.
DeMitchell, T. (2012). In loco parentis. *Education Law, 13,* 36.
F.H., by his next friend Sandra Fay Hall; Sandra Fay Hall v. Memphis City Schools; Vincent Hunter; Walter Banks; Malica Johnson; Patricia A. Toarmina; Pat Beane. U.S. Court of Appeals for the 6th Circuit. (September 4, 2014).
Herrera ex rel. Estate of I.H. v. Hillsborough County Sch. Board, 6 IDELR 137 (MD. Florida 2013).
Individuals with Disabilities Education Improvement Act (IDEA) of 2004, PL 108-446, 20 U.S.C. §§ 1400 *et seq.*
Johns, B., & Carr, V. (2009). *Techniques for managing verbally and physically aggressive students* (3rd ed.). Denver, CO: Love Publishing.
Kok ex rel. Estate of Kok v. Tacoma Sch. Dist. No. 10, 62 IDELR 89 (Wash. Ct. App. 2013).
Payne ex rel. D.P. v. Peninsula Sch. Dist., 61 IDELR 279 (W.D. Wash. 2013).
Slater, A. (2014). *The special education 2014 desk book.* Palm Beach Gardens, FL: LRP Publications.
U.S. Department of Education. (2014, October 21). *Dear colleague letter.* Washington, DC: Author.

CHAPTER 6

Anaheim Union High Sch. Dist. v. J.E., 61 IDELR 107 (C.D. Cal. 2013).
Cortiella, C. (2011). *The state of learning disabilities.* New York, NY: National Center for Learning Disabilities.
Individuals with Disabilities Education Act Regulations, 34 C.F.R. 300.115.
Individuals with Disabilities Education Act Regulations, 34 C.F.R. 300.324.
Individuals with Disabilities Education Act Regulations, 34 C.F.R. 300.524.
Individuals with Disabilities Education Act Regulations, 34 C.F.R. 300.530.
Individuals with Disabilities Education Act Regulations, 34 C.F.R. 300.531.
Individuals with Disabilities Education Act Regulations, 34 C.F.R. 300.532.
Individuals with Disabilities Education Act Regulations, 34 C.F.R. 300.534.
Individuals with Disabilities Education Act Regulations, 34 C.F.R. 300.536.

Individuals with Disabilities Education Improvement Act (IDEA) of 2004, PL 108-446, 20 U.S.C. §§ 1400 *et seq.*

Johns, B. (2014). *Getting behavioral interventions right: Proper uses to avoid common abuses.* Palm Beach Gardens, FL: LRP Publications.

Johns, B., & Carr, V. (2012). *Reduction of school violence: Alternatives to suspension.* Palm Beach Gardens, FL: LRP publications.

Lerner, J., & Johns, B. (2015). *Learning disabilities and related disabilities: Strategies for success (13th ed.).* Stamford, CT: Cengage.

Lewin, T. (2012, March 6). Black students face more discipline, data suggests. *New York Times.* Retrieved from http://www.nytimes.com/2012/03/06/education/black-students-face-more-harsh-discipline-data. In print "Black Students Punished More, Data Suggests," page A11.

O'Connor, K., & Stichter, J. (2011). Using problem-solving frameworks to address challenging behavior of students with high-functioning autism and/or Asperger syndrome. *Beyond Behavior, 20*(1), 11–17.

U.S. Department of Education. (2014, October 21). *Dear colleague letter.* Washington, DC: Author.

U.S. Department of Justice and U.S. Department of Education (2014, January 8). *Dear colleague letter.* Washington, DC: Author.

Wehby, J., & Kern, L. (2014). Intensive behavior intervention: What is it, what is its evidence base, and why do we need to implement now? *Teaching Exceptional Children, 46*(4), 38–44.

CHAPTER 7

Cornell, D., & Limber, S.P. (2015). Law and policy on the concept of bullying at school. *American Psychologist, 70*(4), 333–343.

Family Educational Rights and Privacy Act (FERPA) of 1974, PL 93-380, 20 U.S.C. §§ 1232g *et seq.*

Family Educational Rights and Privacy Act Regulations, 34 C.F.R. 99.10.

Individuals with Disabilities Education Act Regulations, 34 C.F.R. 300.300.

Individuals with Disabilities Education Act Regulations, 34 C.F.R. 300.306.

Individuals with Disabilities Education Act Regulations, 34 C.F.R. 300.311.

Individuals with Disabilities Education Act Regulations, 34 C.F.R. 300.322.

Individuals with Disabilities Education Act Regulations, 34 C.F.R. 300.503.

Individuals with Disabilities Education Act Regulations, 34 C.F.R. 300.505.

Individuals with Disabilities Education Act Regulations, 34 C.F.R. 300.624.

Individuals with Disabilities Education Improvement Act (IDEA) of 2004, PL 108-446, 20 U.S.C. §§ 1400 *et seq.*

Scruggs v. Meriden Bd. of Educ., 48 IDELR 158 (D. Conn. 2007).

Shipley, A. (2014, November 25). *Miramar grade-fixing for football players 'improper' district says.* Retrieved from www.sun-sentinel.com/sports/highschool/football/broward/fl-miramar-grade-manipulation-20141125-story.html

CHAPTER 8

20 U.S.C. 1400.

Family Educational Rights and Privacy Act (FERPA) of 1974, PL 93-380, 20 U.S.C. §§ 1232g *et seq.*

Family Educational Rights and Privacy Act Regulations, 34 C.F.R. 99.

Family Educational Rights and Privacy Act Regulations, 34 C.F.R. 99.10.

Health Insurance Portability and Accountability Act (HIPAA) of 1996, PL 104-191, 42 U.S.C. §§ 201 *et seq.*

Individuals with Disabilities Education Act Regulations, 34 C.F.R. 300.613.

Individuals with Disabilities Education Act Regulations, 34 C.F.R. 300.617.

Individuals with Disabilities Education Act Regulations, 34 C.F.R. 300.624.

Individuals with Disabilities Education Improvement Act (IDEA) of 2004, PL 108-446, 20 U.S.C. §§ 1400 *et seq.*

CHAPTER 9

Individuals with Disabilities Education Act Regulations, 34 C.F.R. 300.305.
Individuals with Disabilities Education Act Regulations, 34 C.F.R. 300.320.
Individuals with Disabilities Education Act Regulations, 34 C.F.R. 300.321.
Individuals with Disabilities Education Act Regulations, 34 C.F.R. 300.324.
Individuals with Disabilities Education Act Regulations, 34 C.F.R. 300.502.
Individuals with Disabilities Education Act Regulations, 34 C.F.R. 300.530.
Individuals with Disabilities Education Improvement Act (IDEA) of 2004, PL 108-446, 20 U.S.C. §§ 1400 *et seq.*
Vincent ex rel. B.V. v. Kenosha Unified Sch. Dist., 59 IDELR 242 (E.D. Wis. 2012).

CHAPTER 10

Eckes, S. (2013, September). Strippers, beer, and bachelorette parties. Regulating teachers' out-of-school conduct. *Principal Leadership,* 8–10.
Individuals with Disabilities Education Improvement Act (IDEA) of 2004, PL 108-446, 20 U.S.C. §§ 1400 *et seq.*
Pickering v. Board of Education, 391 U.S. 563 (1968).
Simpson, M. (2010). *Social networking nightmares.* Retrieved from http://www.nea.org/home/38324.htm
Spanierman v. Hughes, 576 F. Supp. 2d 292 (D. Conn. 2008).
Tara L. Richerson v. Jeanne Beckon, in her individual capacity and official capacity as Executive Director of Human Resources for the Central Kitsap School District, U.S. Court of Appeals for the 9th Circuit (2009).
Zirkel, P. (2008). Courtside: MySpace? *Phi Delta Kappan, 90*(5), 388–389.

GLOSSARY

20 U.S.C. Section 1400.
20 U.S.C. Section 1401.
20 U.S.C. Section 1412.
20 U.S.C. Section 1414.
20 U.S.C. Section 1436.
Council for Exceptional Children (2015). *What every special educator must know: Professional ethics and standards. Seventh edition.* Arlington, VA: The Council for Exceptional Children.
Eckes, S. (2013, September). Strippers, beer, and bachelorette parties: Regulating teachers' out-of-school conduct. *Principal Leadership,* 8–10.
Family Educational Rights and Privacy Act, 34 C.F.R. 99.
Family Educational Rights and Privacy Act, 34 C.F.R. 99.10.
Family Educational Rights and Privacy Act, 34 C.F.R. 99.30.
Family Educational Rights and Privacy Act, 34 C.F.R. 99.31.
Family Educational Rights and Privacy Act (FERPA) of 1974, PL 93-380, 20 U.S.C. §§ 1232g *et seq.*
Individuals with Disabilities Education Act Regulations, 34 C.F.R. 300.15.
Individuals with Disabilities Education Act Regulations, 34 C.F.R. 300.17.
Individuals with Disabilities Education Act Regulations, 34 C.F.R. 300.30.
Individuals with Disabilities Education Act Regulations, 34 C.F.R. 300.39.
Individuals with Disabilities Education Act Regulations, 34 C.F.R. 300.42.
Individuals with Disabilities Education Act Regulations, 34 C.F.R. 300.43.
Individuals with Disabilities Education Act Regulations, 34 C.F.R. 300.106.
Individuals with Disabilities Education Act Regulations, 34 C.F.R. 300.107.
Individuals with Disabilities Education Act Regulations, 34 C.F.R. 300.108.
Individuals with Disabilities Education Act Regulations, 34 C.F.R. 300.114.
Individuals with Disabilities Education Act Regulations, 34 C.F.R. 300.115.
Individuals with Disabilities Education Act Regulations, 34 C.F.R. 300.132.
Individuals with Disabilities Education Act Regulations, 34 C.F.R. 300.133.

Individuals with Disabilities Education Act Regulations, 34 C.F.R. 300.156.
Individuals with Disabilities Education Act Regulations, 34 C.F.R. 300.320.
Individuals with Disabilities Education Act Regulations, 34 C.F.R. 300.321.
Individuals with Disabilities Education Act Regulations, 34 C.F.R. 300.322.
Individuals with Disabilities Education Act Regulations, 34 C.F.R. 300.324.
Individuals with Disabilities Education Act Regulations, 34 C.F.R. 300.328.
Individuals with Disabilities Education Act Regulations, 34 C.F.R. 300.530.
Individuals with Disabilities Education Act Regulations, 34 C.F.R. 300.531.
Individuals with Disabilities Education Act Regulations, 34 C.F.R. 300.534.
Individuals with Disabilities Education Act Regulations, 34 C.F.R. 300.536.
Individuals with Disabilities Education Act Regulations, 34 C.F.R. 300.610.
Individuals with Disabilities Education Act Regulations, 34 C.F.R. 300.613.
Individuals with Disabilities Education Act Regulations, 34 C.F.R. 300.624.
Individuals with Disabilities Education Improvement Act (IDEA) of 2004, PL 108-446, 20
    U.S.C. §§ 1400 *et seq.*

Glossary of Key Terms

access rights Each school district "must permit parents to inspect and review any education records relating to their children that are collected, maintained, or used by the agency under this part" (34 C.F.R. 300.613). "The agency must comply with a request for records without unnecessary delay and before any meeting regarding an IEP, or any hearing" (34 C.F.R. 300.613). "If circumstances effectively prevent the parent or eligible student from exercising the right to inspect and review the student's education records" (34 C.F.R. 99.10), the district has to provide the parent or eligible student with a copy of the records requested or make other arrangements for the parent or eligible student to inspect and review those records (34 C.F.R. 99.10).

accommodations Strategies, services, or supports that are provided to the student in curriculum, instruction, and assessment that do not change the content of the material and level the playing field for a student with a disability, including extended time lines (provided that you are not testing ability to complete an assignment within a given amount of time) or a sign language interpreter.

alternative means of meeting participation When conducting individualized education program (IEP) team meetings and placement meetings, "the parent of a child with a disability and a public agency may agree to use alternative means of meeting participation, such as video conferences and conference calls" (34 C.F.R. 300.328).

amendments to the individualized education program (IEP) Changes to the IEP may be made via a formal IEP team meeting or by amending the IEP. A parent of a child with a disability and the local education agency can agree not to convene an IEP meeting for making a change or changes to the IEP and can "develop a written document to amend or modify the child's current IEP" (20 U.S.C. Section 1414).

assistive technology (AT) device "Any item, piece of equipment, or product system, whether acquired commercially off the shelf, modified, or customized that is used to increase, maintain, or improve functional capabilities of a child with a disability" (20 U.S.C. 1401).

assistive technology (AT) service "Any service that directly assists a child with a disability in the selection, acquisition, or use of an assistive technology device" (20 U.S.C. 1401). This service can include an evaluation; purchasing, leasing, or otherwise providing a device; selecting, designing, fitting or adapting a device; coordinating service with assistive technology; training or technical assistance for the child; training or technical assistance for personnel (20 U.S.C. 1401).

basis of knowledge If a child has not been identified as a student with a disability and engages in behavior that is a violation of the code of conduct, then that student can assert any of the protections of the Individuals with Disabilities Education Improvement Act (IDEA) of 2004 (PL 108-446) if school personnel had the basis of knowledge before the behavior that precipitated the disciplinary action, as exhibited by the following:

1. "The parent of the child expressed concern in writing to supervisory or administrative personnel of the appropriate educational agency or a teacher that the child is in need of special education and related services" (34 C.F.R. 300.534).

2. "The parent of the child requested an evaluation of the child" (34 C.F.R. 300.534).

3. "The teacher of the child, or other personnel, had expressed specific concerns about a pattern of behavior demonstrated by the child directly to the director of special education or other supervisory personnel" (34 C.F.R. 300.534).

There are exceptions, including if the parent refused an evaluation or refused services or if the child was evaluated and determined not to be a student with a disability.

behavior intervention plan (BIP)   An individualized plan that is based on the functional behavioral assessment (FBA) and addresses positive behavior interventions and supports (PBIS) designed to target inappropriate behavior.

case-by-case determination   The process whereby school personnel may consider any unique circumstances on a case-by-case basis when determining whether a change in placement is appropriate for a child with a disability who violates a code of student conduct, as long as the determination made is within the specific discipline regulations of IDEA 2004.

change of placement because of disciplinary removals   A change of placement occurs if the removal of a student with a disability is "for more than ten consecutive school days" (34 C.F.R. 300.536) or "the child has been subjected to a series of removals that constitute a pattern" (34 C.F.R. 300.536).

consideration of special factors   A number of special factors must be considered within the IEP process.

1. Consider using PBIS or other strategies when the child has behaviors that impede his or her learning or that of others.

2. In the case of a child with limited English proficiency, "consider the language needs of the child as those needs relate to the child's IEP" (34 C.F.R. 300.324).

3. "In the case of a child who is blind or visually impaired, provide for instruction in Braille and the use of Braille unless the IEP Team determines, after an evaluation of the child's reading and writing skills, needs, and appropriate reading and writing media (including an evaluation of the child's future needs for instruction in Braille or the use of Braille), that instruction in Braille or the use of Braille is not appropriate for the child" (34 C.F.R. 300.324).

4. "Consider the communication needs of the child, and in the case of a child who is deaf or hard of hearing, consider the child's language and communication needs, opportunities for direct communications with peers and

professional personnel in the child's language and communication mode, academic level, and full range of needs, including opportunities for direct instruction in the child's language and communication mode" (34 C.F.R. 300.324).

5. "Consider whether the child needs assistive technology devices and services" (34 C.F.R. 300.324).

collaboration The process of working together in a partnership with other individuals with whom you have a common purpose of assisting a student. In collaboration, all parties bring expertise to the table and are considered a team.

confidentiality "The protection of the confidentiality of any personally identifiable data, information, and records collected or maintained" (34 C.F.R. 300.610).

consultation The process that involves individuals coming together to work with someone who is considered an expert in the field.

continuum of alternative placements A range of placement options that each school district is required to make available to meet the needs of children with disabilities for special education and related services that "includes the alternative placements listed in the definition of special education under Section 300.68 (instruction in regular classes, special classes, special schools, home instruction, and instruction in hospitals and institutions)" (34 C.F.R. 300.115); "and make provision for supplementary services (such as resource room or itinerant instruction) to be provided in conjunction with regular class placement" (34 C.F.R. 300.115).

co-teaching Two or more teachers (e.g., special education teacher, general education teacher) working together in the general education classroom to deliver instruction to some or all of the students within that classroom.

disclosure "The parent or eligible student shall provide a signed and dated written consent before an educational agency or institution discloses personally identifiable information from the student's education records, except as provided in § 99.31" (34 C.F.R. 99.30). Disclosure can occur to "other school officials, including teachers, within the agency or institution whom the agency or institution has determined to have legitimate educational interests" (34 C.F.R. 99.31). It can also include a consultant or a volunteer who is considered to be performing a service that the district would perform (34 C.F.R. 99.31).

Family Educational Rights and Privacy Act (FERPA) of 1974 (PL 93-380) A federal law that provides for the protections of the right to privacy of students and their families and also provides for the release of information concerning the student.

free appropriate public education (FAPE) Includes special education and related services that are "provided at public expense, under public supervision and direction, and without charge" (34 C.F.R. 300.17) and are "provided in conformity with an individualized education program" (34 C.F.R. 300.17). FAPE also includes the right of students with disabilities ages 3–21 years, including children with disabilities who have been suspended or expelled from school, to receive an education at no cost to the parents or family.

functional behavioral assessment (FBA)   Assessing the "why" of a student's behavior, including the specific function of the behavior. Is the behavior for access to attention or power and control, escape or avoidance, or a sensory reason? It also investigates the ABCs of behavior—what happens before the behavior occurs (antecedents), the specific behavior and a measurable description of the behavior (behavior), and what happens after the behavior occurs (consequences).

IDEA   *See* Individuals with Disabilities Education Improvement Act of 2004.

IEE   *See* independent educational evaluation.

IEP   *See* individualized education program.

IEP team   The group of individuals composed of the parents of the child with a disability; "not less than one regular education teacher of the child if the child is, or may be, participating in the regular education environment" (20 U.S.C. 1414); "not less than one special education teacher, or where appropriate, not less than one special education provider of such child" (20 U.S.C. 1414); "a representative of the local education agency who is (I) qualified to provide, or supervise the provision of specially designed instruction to meet the unique needs of children with disabilities, (II) is knowledgeable about the general education curriculum, and (III) is knowledgeable about the availability of resources of the local educational agency" (20 U.S.C. 1414); "an individual who can interpret the instructional implications of evaluation results, who may be another member of the team;" "at the discretion of the parent or the agency, other individuals who have knowledge or special expertise regarding the child, including related services personnel as appropriate" (20 U.S.C. 1414); and "whenever appropriate, the child with a disability" (20 U.S.C. 1414).

in loco parentis   Schools act in place of the parent or instead of the parent. Schools that take physical custody and control of children are effectively taking the place of their parents and guardians.

independent educational evaluation (IEE)   An evaluation conducted by a qualified examiner who is not employed by the school district who is responsible for the education of the child in question.

individualized education program (IEP)   A written statement for each child with a disability that is developed, reviewed, and revised in an annual meeting. Components of the IEP include a statement of the child's present level of academic achievement and functional performance; a statement of measurable annual goals; a description of how the child's progress toward meeting the goals will be measured; a statement of the special education and related services and supplementary aids and services, based on peer-reviewed research to the extent practicable, to be provided to the child, or on behalf of the child and a statement of program modifications or supports for school personnel; an explanation of the extent, if any, to which the child will not participate with typically developing children in the regular class; "a statement of any individual appropriate accommodations that are necessary to measure the academic achievement and functional performance of the child on state and districtwide assessments..." (34 C.F.R. 300.320); projected dates for the beginning of the services and the frequency, location, and duration of those services and modifications (34 C.F.R. 300.320).

Individuals with Disabilities Education Improvement Act (IDEA) of 2004 (PL 108-446)   Governs the provisions of special education services for students with disabilities.

interim alternative educational setting   A setting determined by the IEP team (34 C.F.R. 300.531) where a student with a disability can be removed if he or she violates a code of student conduct from his or her current placement for not more than 10 consecutive school days to the extent those alternatives are applied to children without disabilities and for additional removals of not more than 10 consecutive school days in that same school year for separate incidents of misconduct "as long as those removals do not constitute a change of placement" (34 C.F.R. 300.530). School personnel may remove a student to an interim alternative educational setting for not more than 45 school days without regard to whether the behavior is determined to be a manifestation of the child's disability if the child "carries a weapon to or possesses a weapon at school, on school premises, or to or at a school function" (34 C.F.R. 300.530) under the jurisdiction of the state or local education agency; "knowingly possesses or uses illegal drugs or sells or solicits the sale of a controlled substance, while at school, on school premises or at a school function" (34 C.F.R. 300.530) or "has inflicted serious bodily injury upon another person while at school, on school premises, or at a school function under the jurisdiction of an SEA or an LEA" (34 C.F.R. 300.530).

The interim alternative educational setting must meet these criteria: It must enable the child to continue to participate in the general education curriculum and must allow the student to make progress toward meeting the goals set out in his or her IEP.

least restrictive environment (LRE)   Requires that each public agency must ensure that "to the maximum extent appropriate, children with disabilities, including children in public or private institutions or other care facilities are educated with children who are non-disabled" (34 C.F.R. 300.114); and "special classes, separate schooling, or other removal of children with disabilities from the regular educational environment occurs only if the nature or severity of the disability is such that education in regular classes with the use of supplementary aids and services cannot be achieved satisfactorily" (34 C.F.R. 300.114).

manifestation determination   Within 10 school days of any decision to change the placement of a child with a disability, the IEP team must review all relevant information in the student's file, including the child's IEP, any teacher observations, and any relevant information provided by the parents to determine if the conduct in question was caused by or had a direct and substantial relationship to the child's disability or if the conduct in question was the direct result of the local school district's failure to implement the IEP.

modifications   Changes to the content of the general education curriculum, instruction, or assessment, including off grade-level material or reduced content.

multidisciplinary   Evaluations and placement decisions are made by a team of individuals. It is necessary to have the representation from a variety of professions, including education, psychology, counseling, speech-language pathology, occupational therapy, or nursing, when conducting an evaluation.

multidisciplinary evaluation   An evaluation done by a group of individuals holding a range of positions from a variety of disciplines that is conducted at least every 3 years to "determine whether the child has a disability and the nature and extent of the special education and related services that the child needs" (34 C.F.R. 300.15).

mutually agreeable times   Times established for IEP or other meetings based on the schedules of the school and parent.

nexus theory   This theory "suggests that a teacher's off-duty conduct might have a negative impact on his or her teaching effectiveness" (Eckes, 2013, p. 8).

notice to the parent   Notice to the parent about the IEP meeting must indicate "the purpose, time, and location of the meeting and who will be in attendance" (34 C.F.R. 300.322). "For a child with a disability beginning not later than the first IEP to be in effect when the child turns 16, or younger if determined appropriate by the IEP team, the notice must also (i) indicate that a purpose of the meeting will be the consideration of the post-secondary goals and transition services for the child" (34 C.F.R. 300.322); "the agency will invite the student; (ii) identify any other agency that will be invited to send a representative" (34 C.F.R. 300.322). Please be advised that some states have an earlier requirement for transition plans.

paraprofessionals   Paraprofessionals, or teaching assistants, are those individuals "who are appropriately trained and supervised in accordance with state law, regulation, or written policy, in meeting the requirements of this part to be used to assist in the provision of special education and related services under this part to children with disabilities" (34 C.F.R. 300.156).

parent   Meaning

1.   A biological or adoptive parent of a child

2.   A foster parent, unless state law, regulations, or contractual obligations with a state or local entity prohibit a foster parent from acting as a parent

3.   A guardian generally authorized to act as the child's parent or authorized to make educational decisions for the child (but not the state if the child is a ward of the state)

4.   "An individual acting in the place of a natural or adoptive parent (including a grandparent, stepparent, or other relative) with whom the child lives, or an individual who is legally responsible for the child's welfare" (20 U.S.C. 1401)

5.   A surrogate parent who has been appointed (20 U.S.C. 1401)

States have specific laws and regulations about who is the parent, who is the custodial parent, and the role of the noncustodial parent, so it is important to also know your state laws and regulations.

parent-informed consent   The process in which parents have been fully informed about their special education rights by school personnel before they give written permission for an initial evaluation, specific services, and any reevaluation.

parent-initiated evaluations   Parents always have the right to seek an independent evaluation at their own expense to determine the needs of their child. That evaluation must be considered by the public agency and can be utilized as evidence in any hearing that may occur.

parent participation   The active and informed participation of parents in the evaluation and placement process and in ongoing communication through regularly scheduled parent conferences and progress reports.

parent right to review records   Refers to the parents' ability to review all school records, both temporary and permanent, and receive a copy of those records.

parental concerns   The concerns that parents have for enhancing their child's education must be discussed as a part of every IEP.

parental involvement in evaluation   Parents should be interviewed as part of an evaluation and should be an integral part of that evaluation. Family background, medical history, and other important information about how the child performs at home must be included.

parental involvement in placement   Parents are an active participant in the IEP process in which the school seeks input from parents throughout the meeting and asks for any parental concerns. Parents are provided with the opportunity to observe placement options that may be discussed, to assist with the development of possible goals and objectives, and are provided a draft of the IEP if one is developed by school personnel.

parental right to an independent evaluation at public expense   When parents disagree with the evaluation that school district personnel have completed, the parents have the right to request an independent educational evaluation for their child and the district must either pay for the evaluation or take the parents to due process to determine whether the school district evaluation was appropriate.

permanent records   A permanent record consists of "a student's name, address, and phone number, his or her grades, attendance record, classes attended, grade level completed, and year completed" (34 C.F.R. 300.624). A permanent record is "maintained without time limitation" (34 C.F.R. 300.624).

positive behavior interventions and supports (PBIS)   A multi-tiered system of behavioral interventions in which a universal system of positive recognition for appropriate behavior is established for all students, secondary interventions are designed for those students who need more than the universal system provides, and tertiary interventions are put into place for the small percentage of students who do not respond to either Tier 1 or Tier 2 interventions and are in need of a highly individualized program that can include a case study evaluation to determine whether the student needs special education services.

prior written notice   Written notice provided to the parent in advance of a proposal to initiate an evaluation, initiate placement or change placement, or refuse to initiate an evaluation or placement.

procedural safeguards   Procedural safeguards are a set of rights for parents based on IDEA 2004, and they include the right to due process, the rights of parents to be active participants in the process of the student's education as a student with a disability, including the right to an evaluation, the right to review and have access to student records, the right to be involved in the IEP, the right to receive regularly scheduled progress reports, and the opportunity to present and resolve complaints. Procedural safeguards must be written in easily understandable language and provide protections to parents and children.

records custodian The individual designated within the school district who maintains student records and knows where all of the records on a student are located.

right to know Those individuals within the school system who have been determined to have legitimate educational interests in the student's records and are required to have access to certain information about a student.

response to intervention (RTI) A multi-tiered approach to intervention designed to identify and support students with learning disabilities or those at risk. There are at least three levels—universal instruction, targeted, small-group intervention, and individualized, intensive intervention.

special education "Specially designed instruction, at no cost to the parents, to meet the unique needs of a child with a disability, including (i) instruction conducted in the classroom, in the home, in hospitals and institutions, and in other settings; and (ii) instruction in physical education" (34 C.F.R. 300.39). It also includes each of the following, if needed: "(i) Speech-language pathology services, or any other related service, if the service is considered special education rather than a related service under state standards; (ii) Travel training, and (iii) Vocational education" (34 C.F.R. 300.39).

specially designed instruction Instruction that is based on the individual needs of the child and may result in a change in content, methodology, or delivery of instruction. It ensures access to the general curriculum so that the child can meet the educational standards that apply to all students within the district. It means "to address the unique needs of the child that result from the child's disability" (34 C.F.R. 300.39).

supervision This additional element of in loco parentis refers to the responsibility of educators to monitor the educational environment for the safety and security of the students.

supplementary aids and services "Aids, services, and other supports that are provided in regular education classes, other education-related settings, and in extracurricular and nonacademic settings, to enable children with disabilities to be educated with nondisabled children to the maximum extent appropriate" (34 C.F.R. 300.42).

temporary record Educational records, including special education records, that are released to the parent or the student or destroyed after proper notice once a student exits the school system. States have established specific rules on the removal of records that are kept at least 5 years and consist of such items as special education evaluations, IEPs, and discipline records. Upon notice to the student and family, the student has the right to his or her own records when he or she exits the school system.

transfer of rights at age of majority   "Beginning not later than one year before the child reaches the age of majority under State law, the IEP must include a statement that the child has been informed of the child's rights under Part B of the Act, if any that will transfer to the child on reaching the age of majority" (34 C.F.R. 300.320).

transition services   "A coordinated set of activities for a child with a disability that (1) is designed to be within a results-oriented process, that is focused on improving the academic and functional achievement of the child with a disability to facilitate the child's movement from school to post-school activities, including post-secondary education, vocational education, integrated employment (including supported employment), continuing and adult education, adult services, independent living, or community participation; (2) is based on the individual child's needs, taking into account the child's strengths, preferences, and interests and includes—(i) instruction; (ii) related services; (iii) community experiences; (iv) the development of employment and other post-school adult living objectives; (v) if appropriate, acquisition of daily living skills and provision of a functional vocational evaluation" (34 C.F.R. 300.43). Transition services for children with disabilities "may be special education, if provided as specially designed instruction, or a related service, if required to assist a child with a disability to benefit from special education" (34 C.F.R. 300.43).

transition services participants   When conducting a transition plan, the school "must invite a child with a disability to attend his or her IEP if a purpose of the meeting will be the consideration of the post-secondary goals for the child and the transition services needed" (34 C.F.R. 300.321). "To the extent appropriate, with the consent of the parents or a child who has reached the age of majority, the public agency must invite a representative of any participating agency that is likely to be responsible for providing or paying for transition services" (34 C.F.R. 300.321).

travel training   "Instruction, as appropriate, to children with significant intellectual disabilities and any other children with disabilities who require this instruction to enable them to (i) Develop an awareness of the environment in which they live; and (ii) Learn the skills necessary to move effectively and safely from place to place within that environment; e.g., in school, in the home, at work, and in the community" (34 C.F.R. 300.39).

unilateral action   Refers to a decision taken by one person without consulting with the IEP team.

written parental consent for the release of information   Any written consent must be signed and dated and must specify the records to be disclosed, state the purpose of the disclosure, and identify the party or class of parties to whom the disclosure may be made (FERPA and 34 C.F.R. 99).

Appendix

Answer Key for Extras and Activities

CHAPTER 1

How Many Acronyms Do You Know?

FAPE—free appropriate public education

LRE—least restrictive environment

IEP—individualized education program

IDEA—Individuals with Disabilities Education Act

Wheel of Fortune Game

1. Due process

2. Least restrictive environment

3. Free appropriate public education

4. Accommodations

5. Modifications

6. Discrimination

Two Truths and a Lie

Read all of these statements. Two are true, and one is a lie. Determine which one is a lie.

1. The IEP not only determines what the individual child needs but also what supports the teacher may need.

2. According to the Supreme Court in *Honig v. Doe* (1988), schools can suspend students with disabilities for 10 days each time the student is suspended.

3. Schools are expected to provide any medical services other than what a physician would be required to provide.

Answer: 2 is the lie. *Honig v. Doe* (1988) stated that schools could suspend students with disabilities for 10 days per year, not 10 days each time the student misbehaves.

CHAPTER 2

Two Truths and a Lie

Read all of these statements. Two are true, and one is a lie. Determine which one is a lie.

1. If the parents can only come to an IEP meeting on Saturday, then the school must schedule the IEP on Saturday.

2. Under certain circumstances, the school can hold an IEP meeting if the parent cannot attend.

3. Parental concerns must be addressed at the IEP meeting.

Answer: 1 is the lie. The IEP meeting should be held at a mutually agreed upon time and place. Convening on Saturday is probably not mutually agreeable with school staff.

CHAPTER 3

Two Truths and a Lie

Read all of these statements. Two are true, and one is a lie. Determine which one is a lie.

1. The special education teacher's opinion weighs the heaviest on the IEP team because the special educator has expertise in the IEP.
2. The paraprofessional is not responsible for planning instruction for the student.
3. There must be an administrator on every IEP team who is able to approve services.

Answer: 1 is the lie. The special education teacher is a partner in the IEP process, and one individual's opinion does not count more than other school-based team participants.

CHAPTER 4

Two Truths and a Lie

Read all of these statements. Two are true, and one is a lie. Determine which one is a lie.

1. You should have three forms of written documentation to show that you have invited the parent to the IEP meeting.
2. If the parent revokes placement outlined in the IEP, then the school district cannot implement the placement.
3. If the general education teacher refuses to serve the student within the general education class, then the IEP team cannot place the student in the class.

Answer: 3 is the lie. The general education teacher does not have the authority to override a group IEP decision. However, the team will want to look closely at what the student will need in order to be successful in that setting and whether there is another general education classroom that may be more appropriate.

CHAPTER 5

Two Truths and a Lie

Read all of these statements. Two are true, and one is a lie. Determine which one is a lie.

1. A teacher who has exhibited intent to harm that could threaten a child's constitutional rights cannot be personally sued, but the school district itself can be sued.
2. Individuals who work within the school district and who work with the student and have a right to know should be informed of critical information about the student.
3. When a paraprofessional engages in harmful actions to the child, such as blowing a whistle in a child's ear, the teacher has the responsibility to stop the behavior.

Answer: 1 is the lie. The teacher can be sued personally, and the school district also can be sued, unless it took steps to stop what the teacher was doing.

CHAPTER 6

How Many of These Acronyms Do You Know?

FBA— functional behavioral assessment

BIP— behavior intervention plan

PBIS—positive behavior interventions and supports

SWPBIS—schoolwide positive behavior interventions and supports

ABC— antecedents, behaviors, consequences

Two Truths and a Lie

Read all of these statements. Two are true, and one is a lie. Determine which one is a lie.

1. Students who bring weapons or drugs to school can be placed in an interim alternative educational setting for 45 school days.

2. Students can be suspended for 10 days at a time.

3. BIPs must be developed for those students with disabilities whose behavior interferes with their learning.

Answer: 2 is the lie. Students can be suspended up to 10 school days per year, including extended school year, without services.

CHAPTER 7

Two Truths and a Lie

Read all of these statements. Two are true, and one is a lie. Determine which one is a lie.

1. A student's attendance records are part of his or her permanent records.

2. A student's discipline records are part of his or her permanent records.

3. All schools have to have an individual designated as a records custodian.

Answer: 2 is the lie. Student discipline records are part of temporary records.

CHAPTER 8

Interact

*   Give each participant two cards—one says "right" and the other says "wrong." Show participants the following statements, and have them raise the correct card—is it right or is it wrong?

    a. Bill, a fifth grader, has diabetes. The cafeteria supervisor has the right to know this information.

    b. A publicly posted list of student grades that identifies each student is permissible as long as it is in the classroom.

    c. A record is anything written down about a student.

    d. Any teacher in a school building has a right to view a student's online IEP.

    e. It is permissible for a public school to send student records to a parochial school without the parents' permission.

    Answers: a: right; b: wrong; c: wrong—only if it is shared with anyone; d: wrong—only if the teacher is working with the student and has the right to know; e: wrong

*   Get into a group and play a This or That activity. Put two signs up at either side of the room. Put a sign up that says "This" on one side of the room. Put a sign up that says "That" on the other side of the room. "This" denotes permanent records. "That" denotes

temporary records. Read the following phrases, and have participants move to the sign indicating which type of record contains that information.

a.   Birth date

b.   Extracurricular activities

c.   IEPs

d.   Grades

e.   Class standing

f.   Psychological evaluations

Answers: a: this—permanent; b: this—permanent; c: that—temporary; d: this—permanent; e: this—permanent; f: that—temporary

Two Truths and a Lie

Read all of these statements. Two are true, and one is a lie. Determine which one is a lie.

1.   Temporary records include IEPs.

2.   Confidentiality applies only to students within the school.

3.   Nothing that denotes special education should be referred to in a permanent record.

Answer: 2 is the lie. Confidentiality also applies to staff members.

CHAPTER 9

Interact

- Give each participant two cards—one that says "yes" and one that says "no." Ask whether unilateral action is allowed for the following decisions. Participants raise their card with the appropriate answer.

  a.   The principal decides what testing accommodations can be given.

  b.   The teacher changes the amount of time a student sees the SLP.

  c.   The teacher sends a student home for the rest of the day because of the student's behavior.

  d.   The teacher changes the order of when reading and math take place on one day.

  e.   The principal determines that an independent evaluation that a parent had done is not important.

Answers: a: no; b: no; c: no; d: yes; e: no

Two Truths and a Lie

Read all of these statements. Two are true, and one is a lie. Determine which one is a lie.

1.   School personnel may unilaterally suspend a student for not more than 10 school days.

2.   School district personnel who are requesting an IEP meeting that includes developing a transition plan do not have to invite a representative of an agency that provides post-school services if they do not believe the agency representative will attend anyway.

3.   The school principal should invite a classroom teacher to the IEP even though the student is placed in a specialized school.

Answer: 2 is the lie. The district must invite the agency representative even if it is likely the individual will not attend.

CHAPTER 10

Two Truths and a Lie

Read all of these statements. Two are true, and one is a lie. Determine which one is a lie.

1. Off-duty conduct can be considered when determining whether an individual should be reemployed.

2. What a school district employee posts on Facebook is no business of the school district.

3. Educators are not always protected by the Constitution's First Amendment of freedom of speech.

Answer: 2 is the lie. A school district does have the right to review and take action against someone who posts inappropriate comments on Facebook.

Index